Ten Preludes

Op.1

1-10

By: Dubiell A De Zarraga Lago

www.lulu.com/dubiell

2010 De Zarraga Lago,Dubiell,A.

978-0-557-72972-2All Right Reserved

www.dezarragadubiell@yahoo.com

Prelude No.1

Dubiell De Zarraga Lago

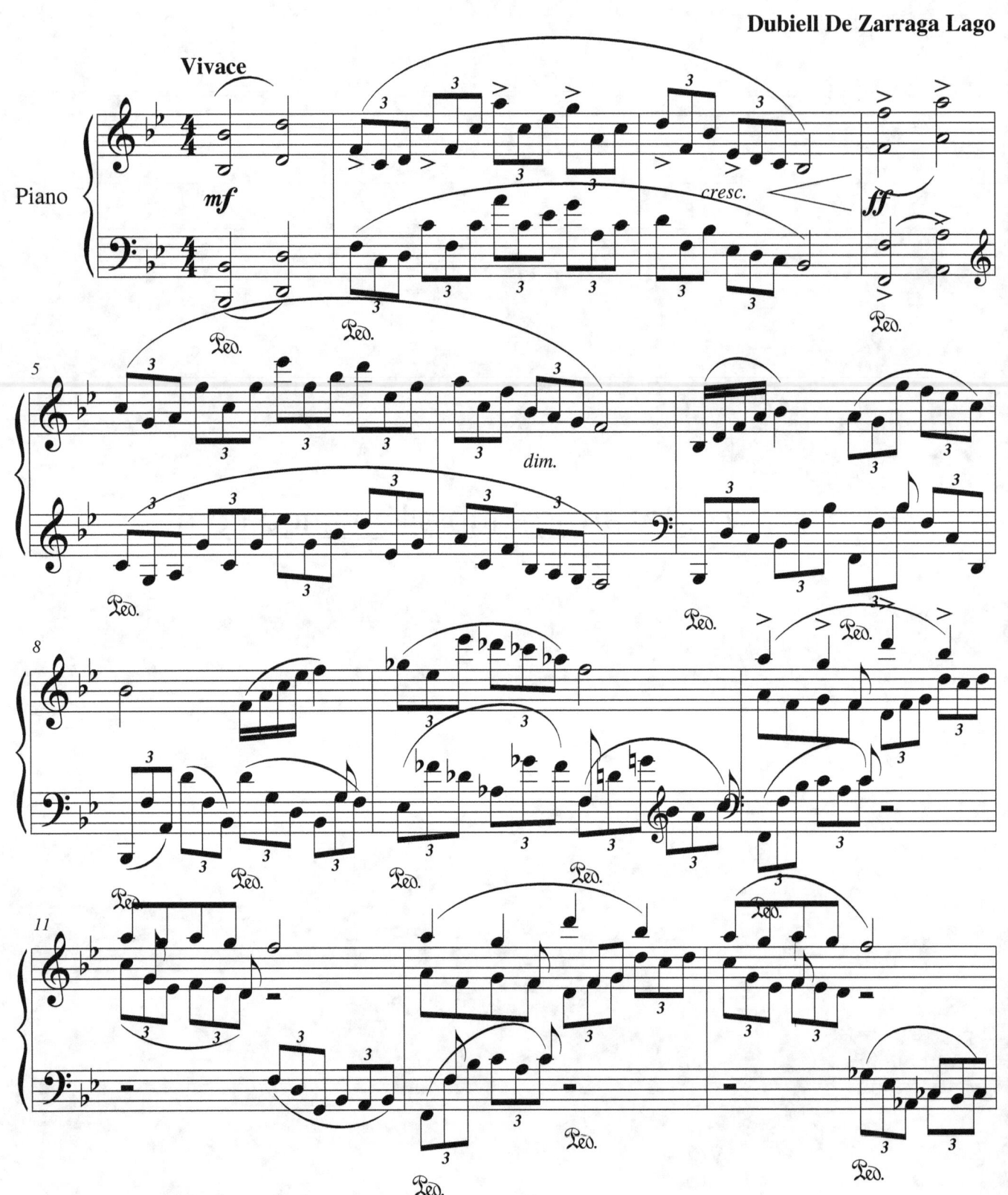

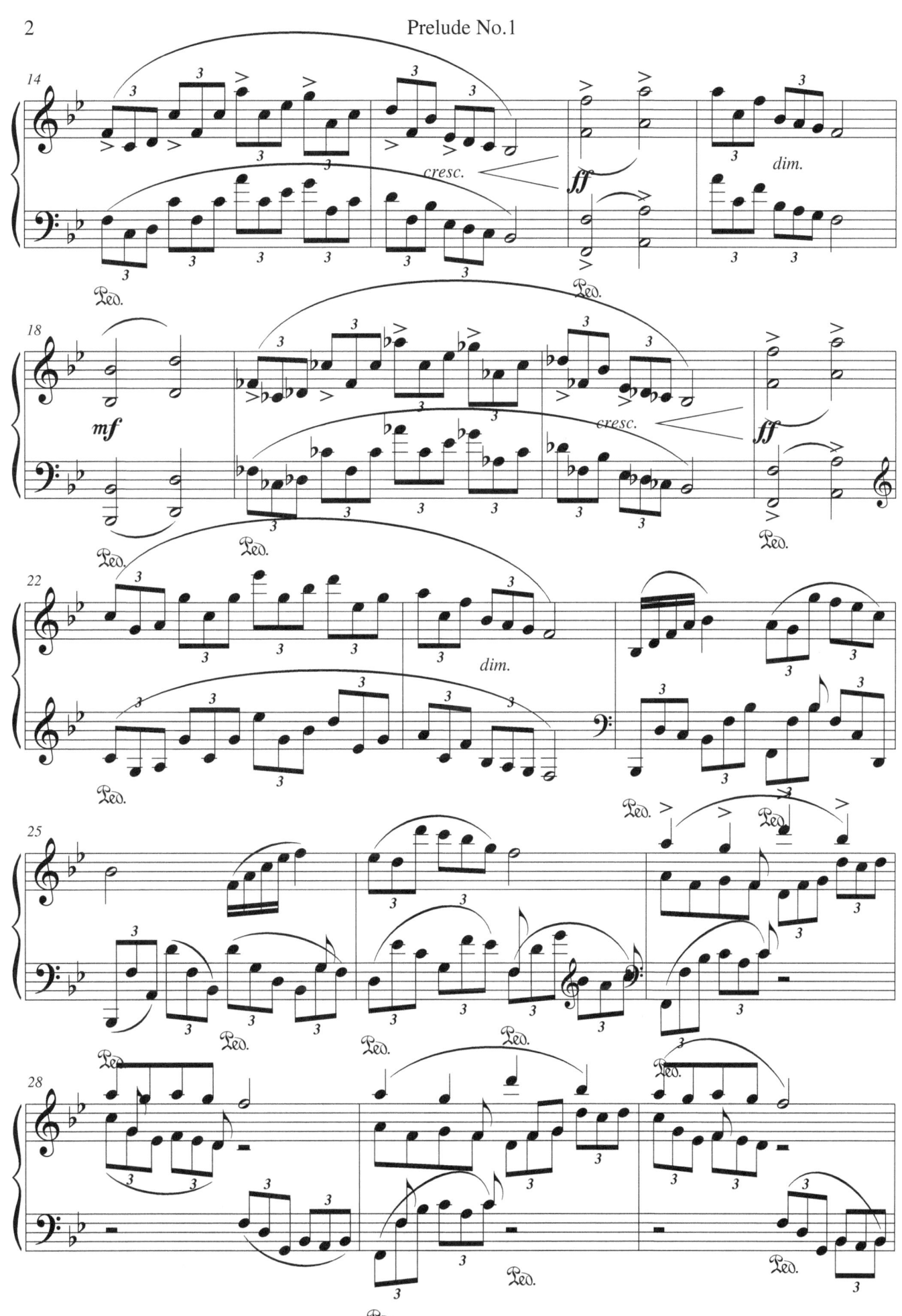

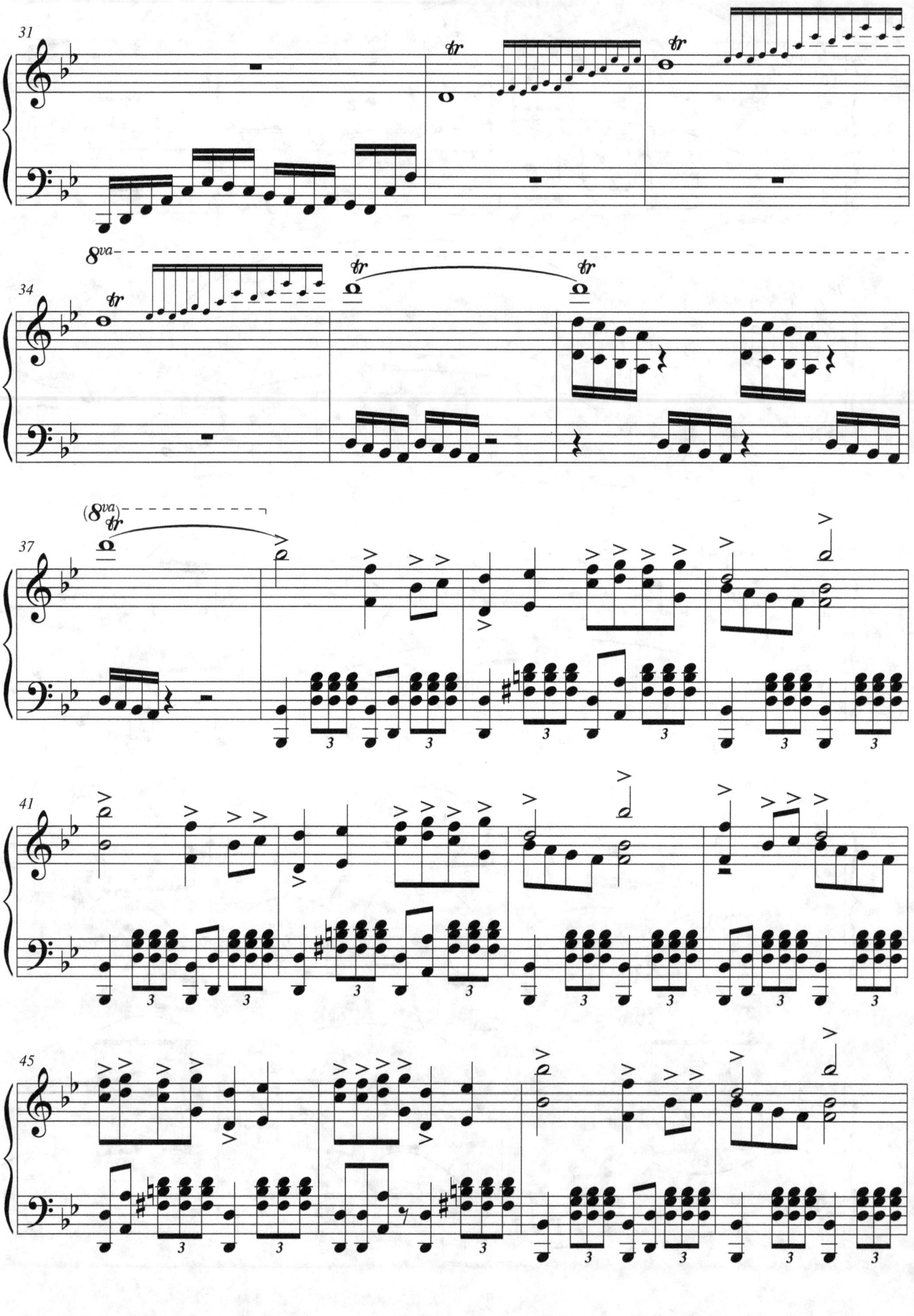

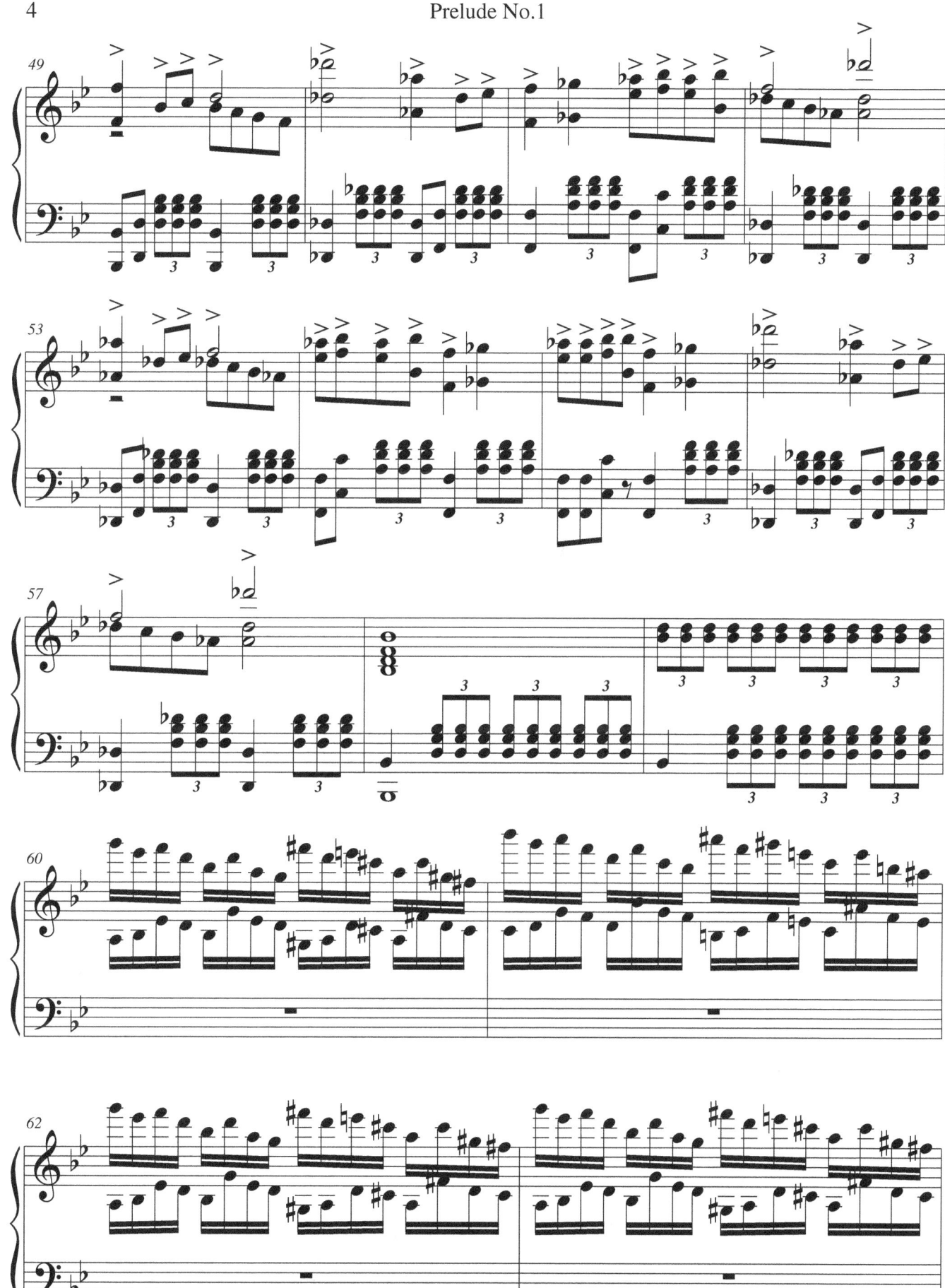

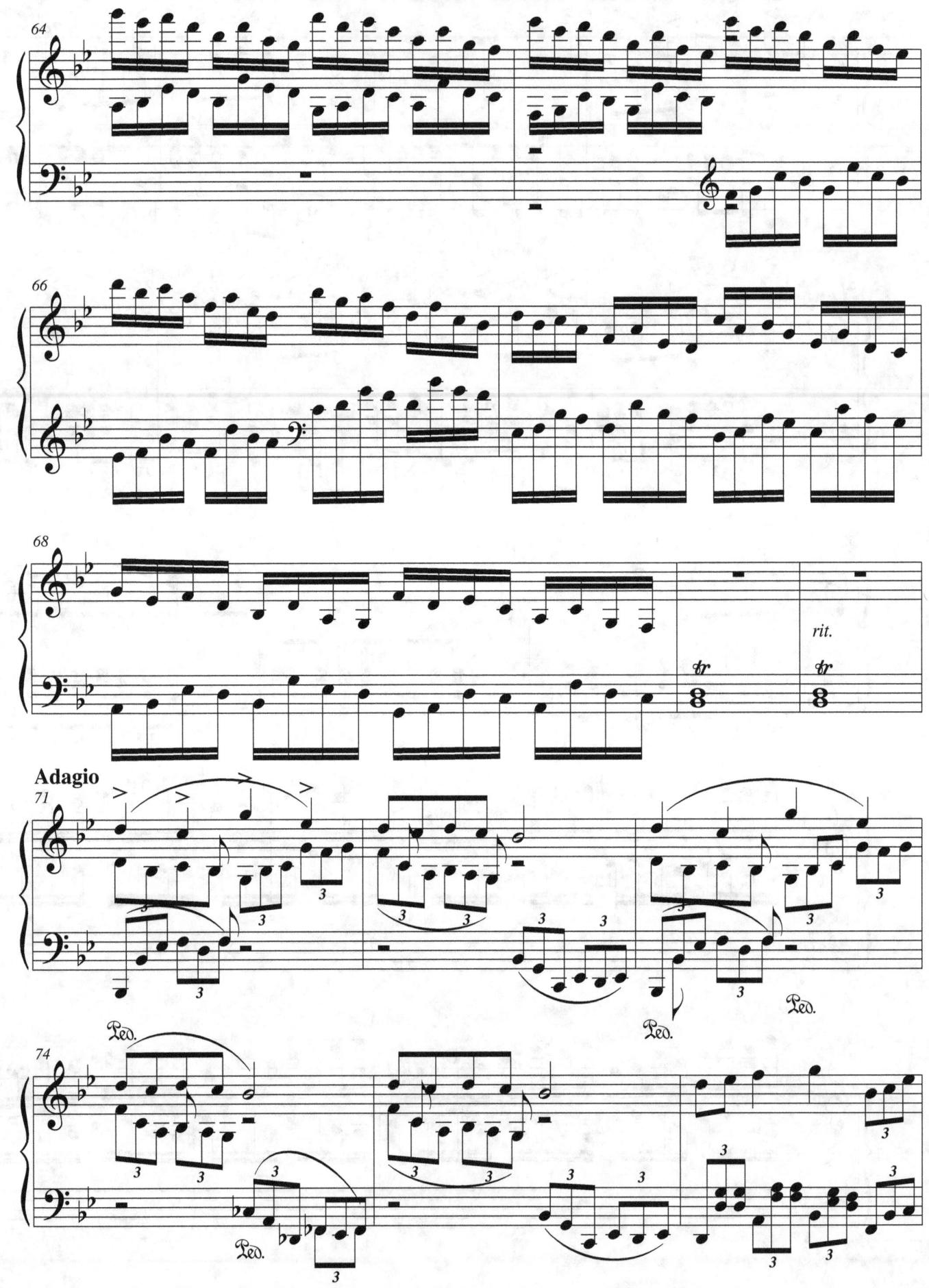

Prelude No.1

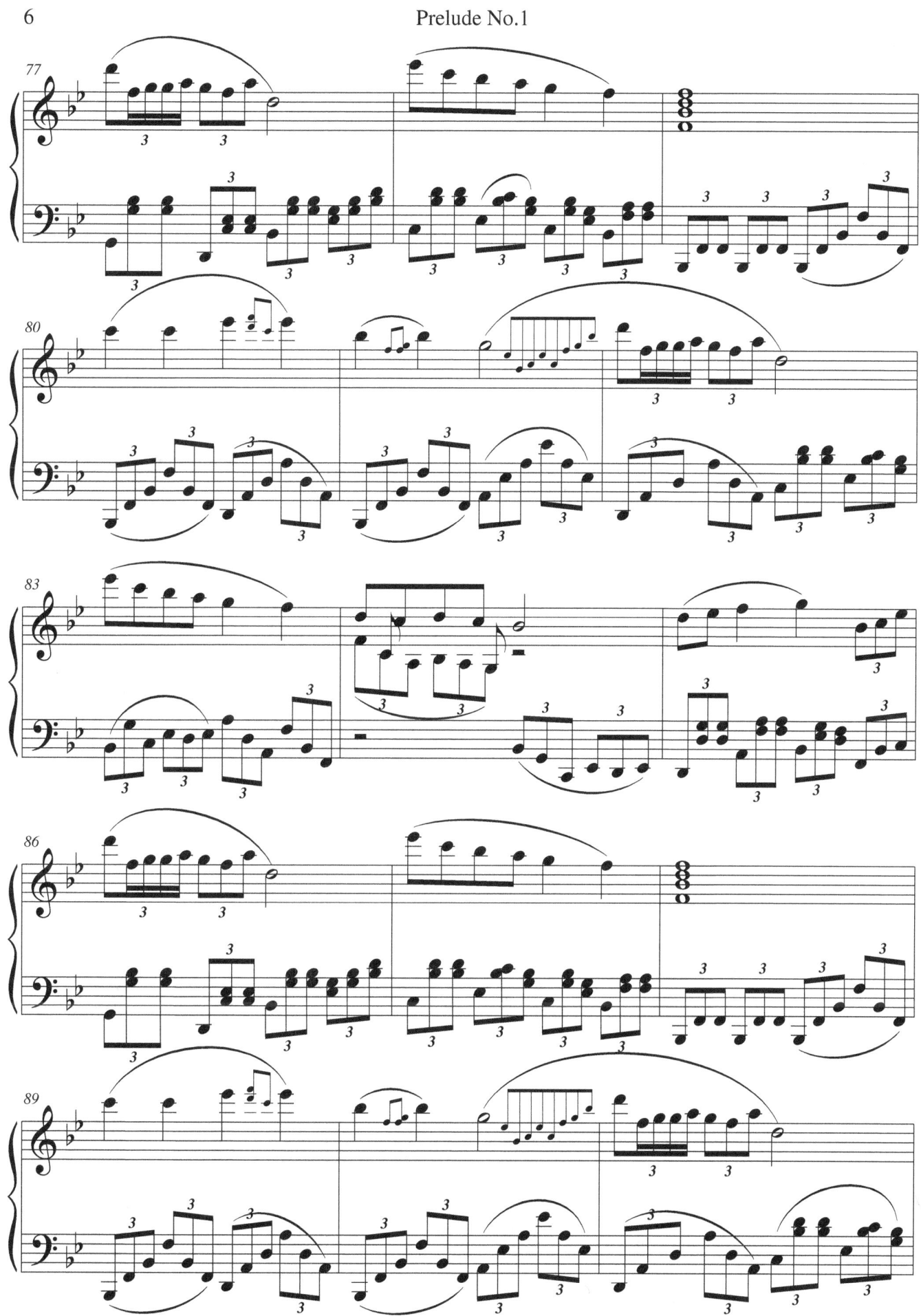

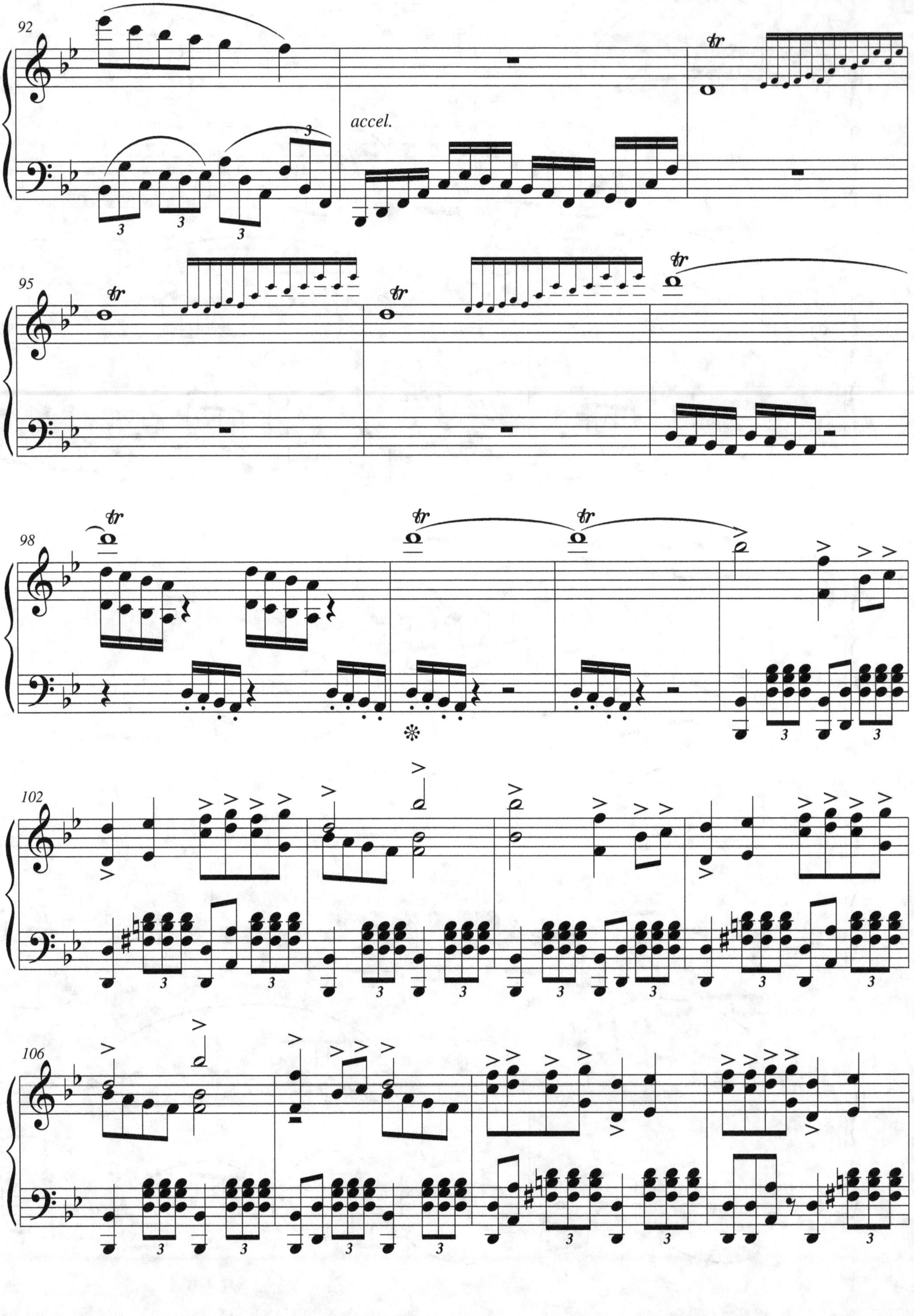

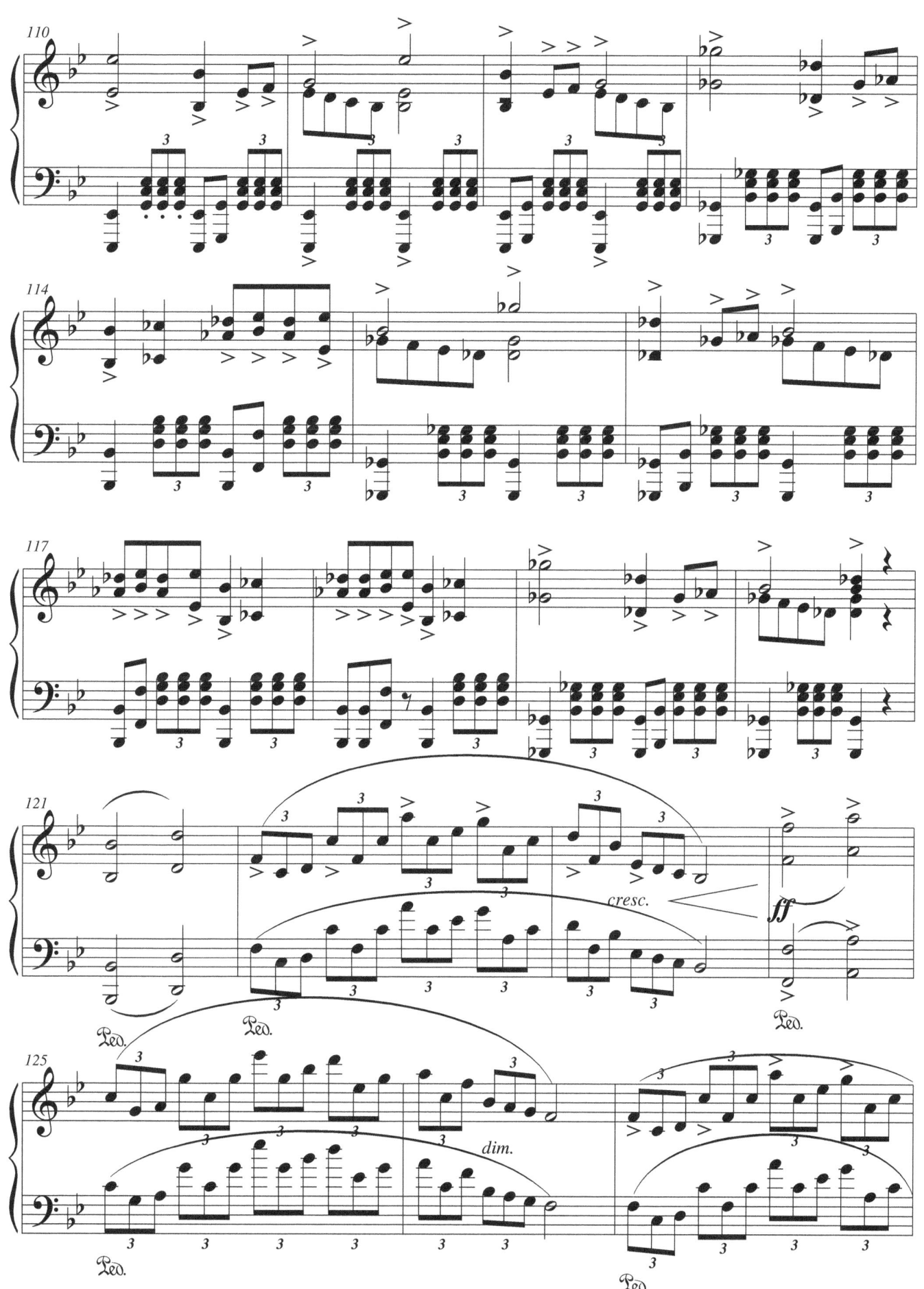

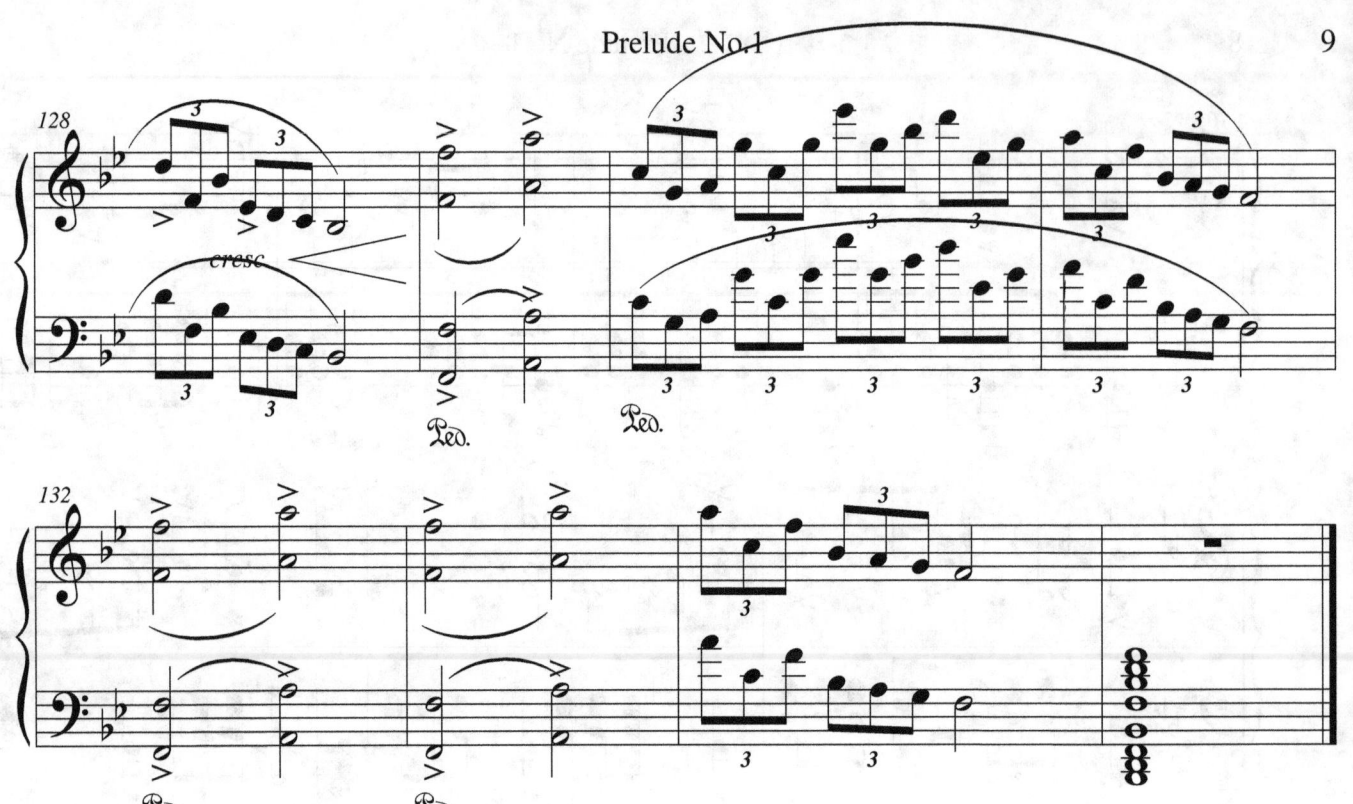

Prelude No.2

Dubiell De Zarraga

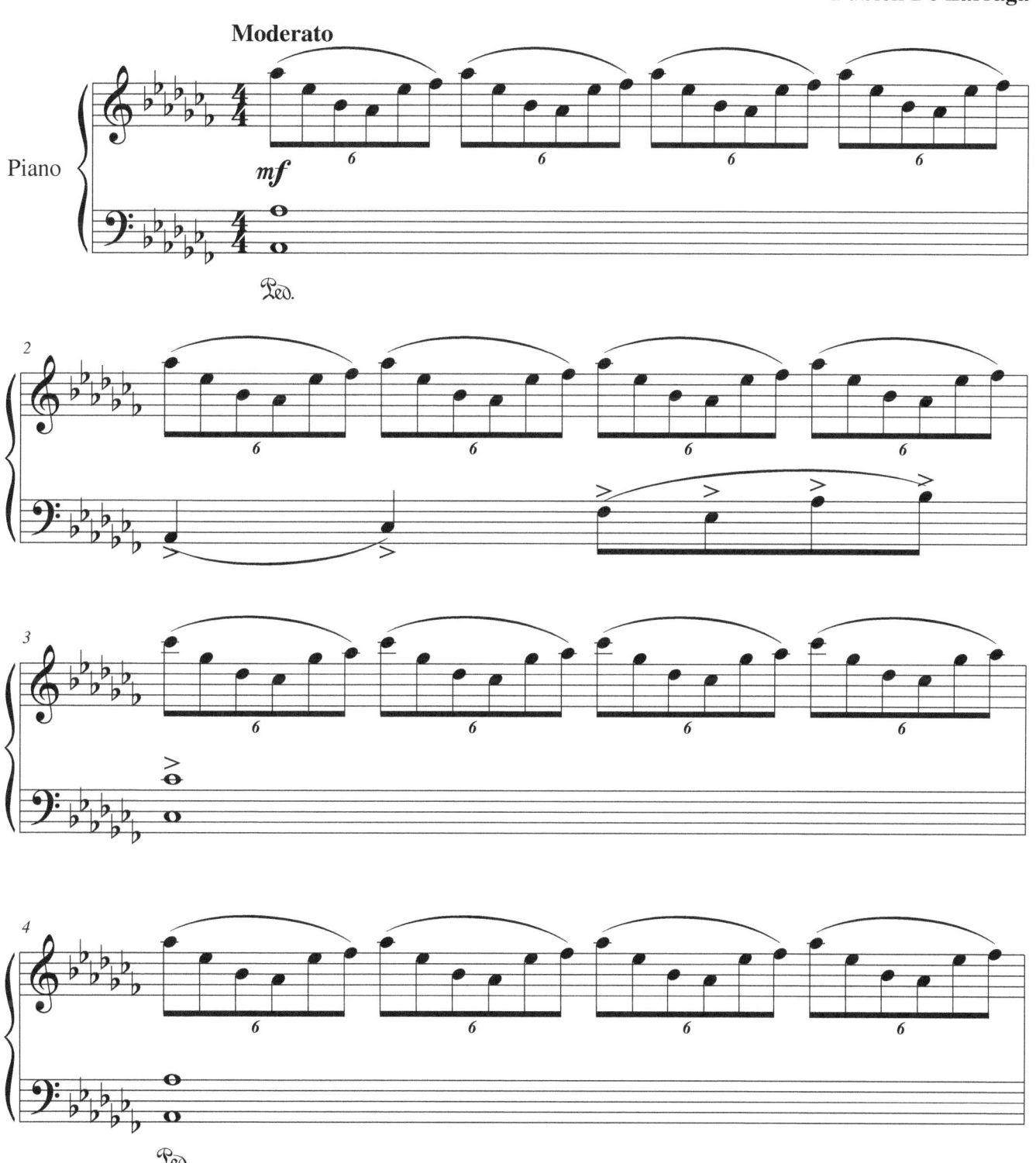

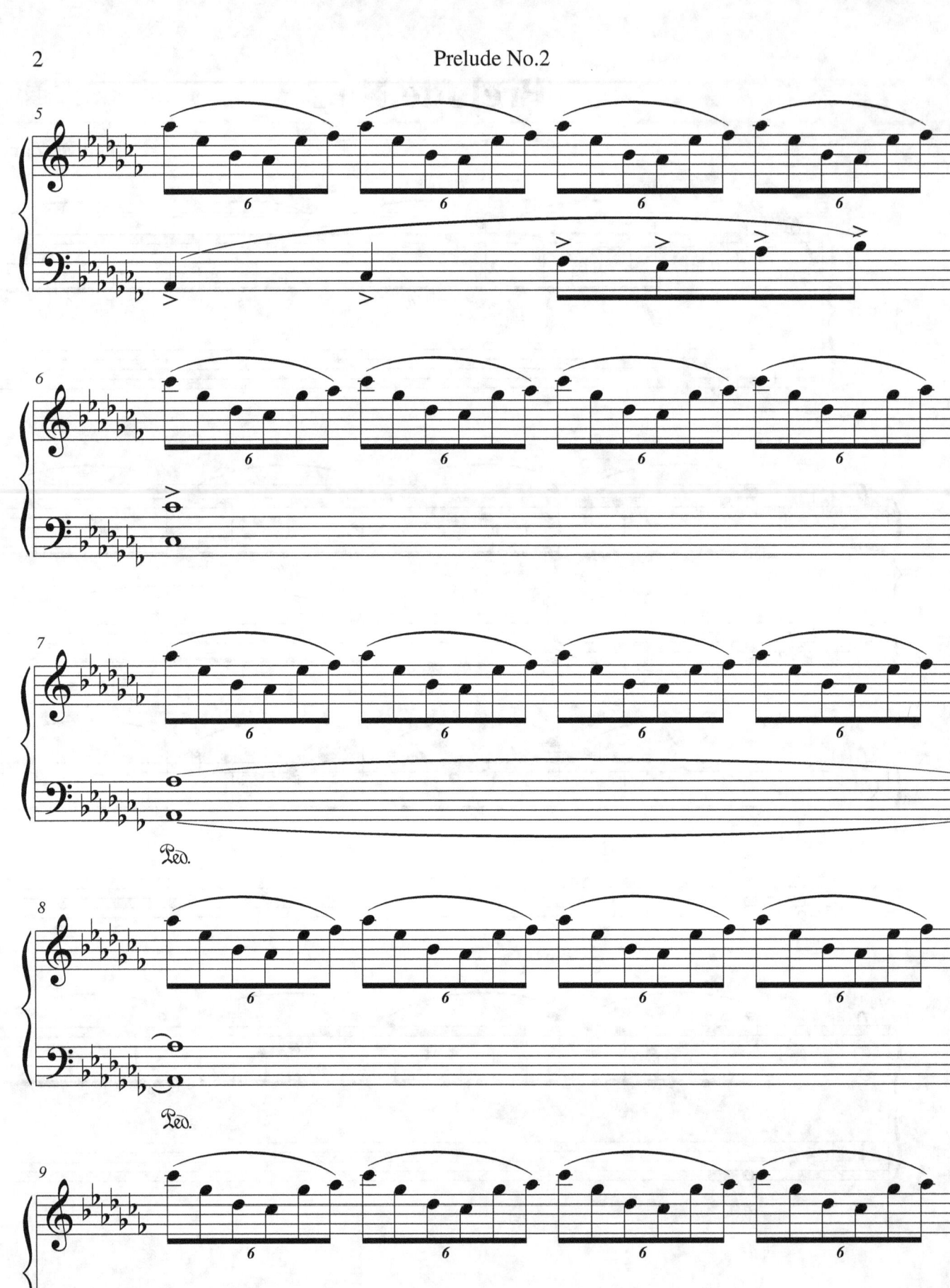

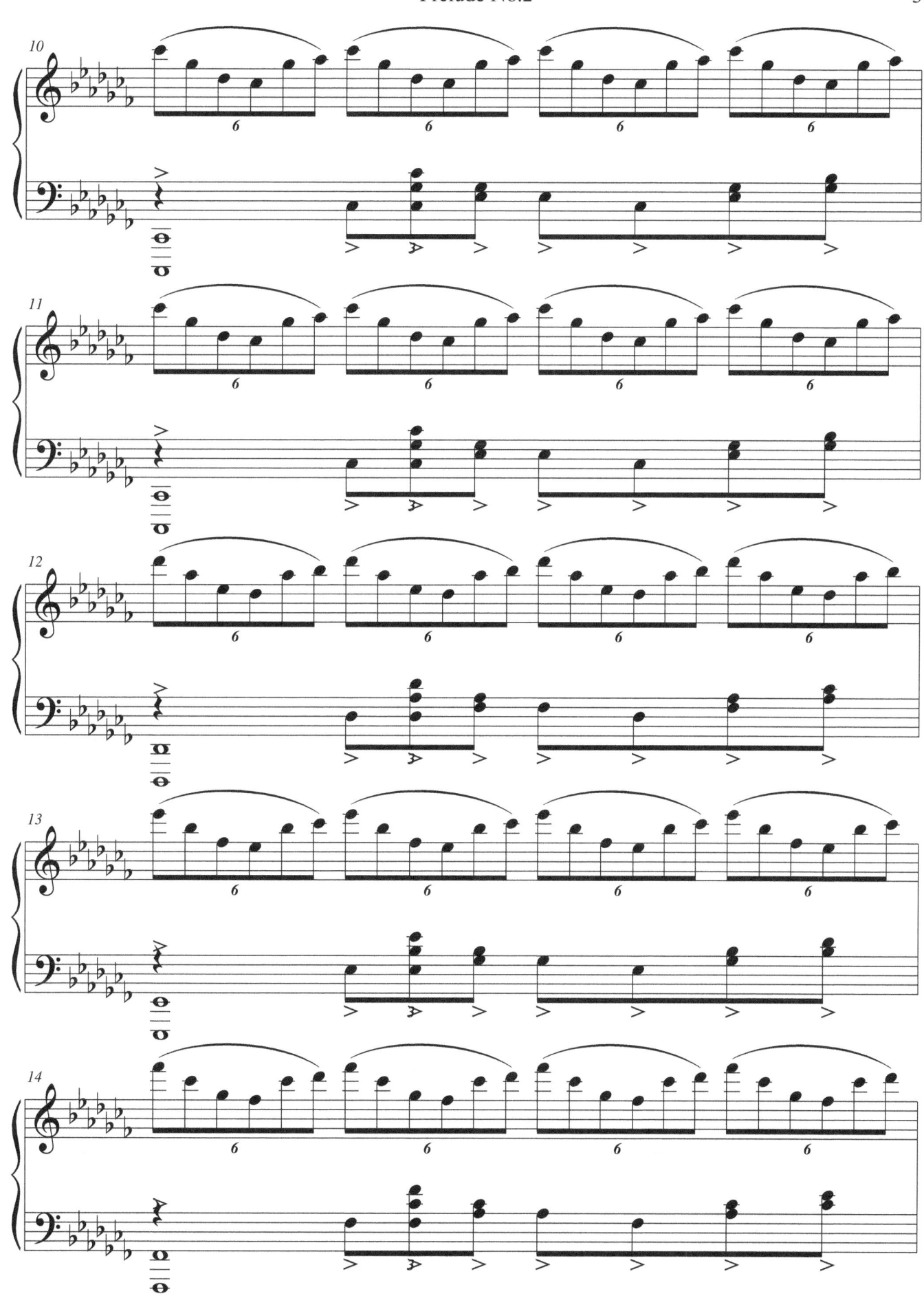

Prelude No.2

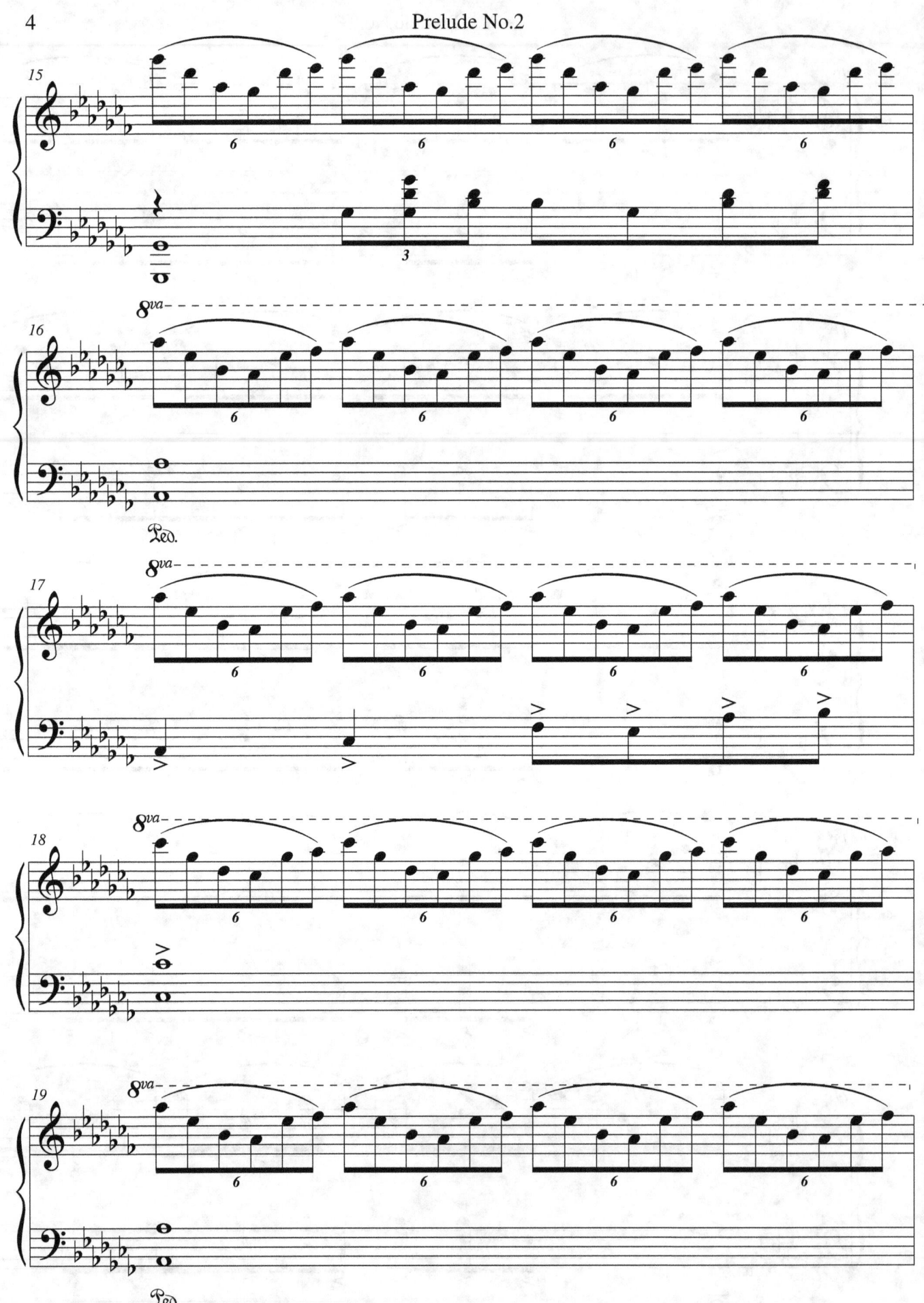

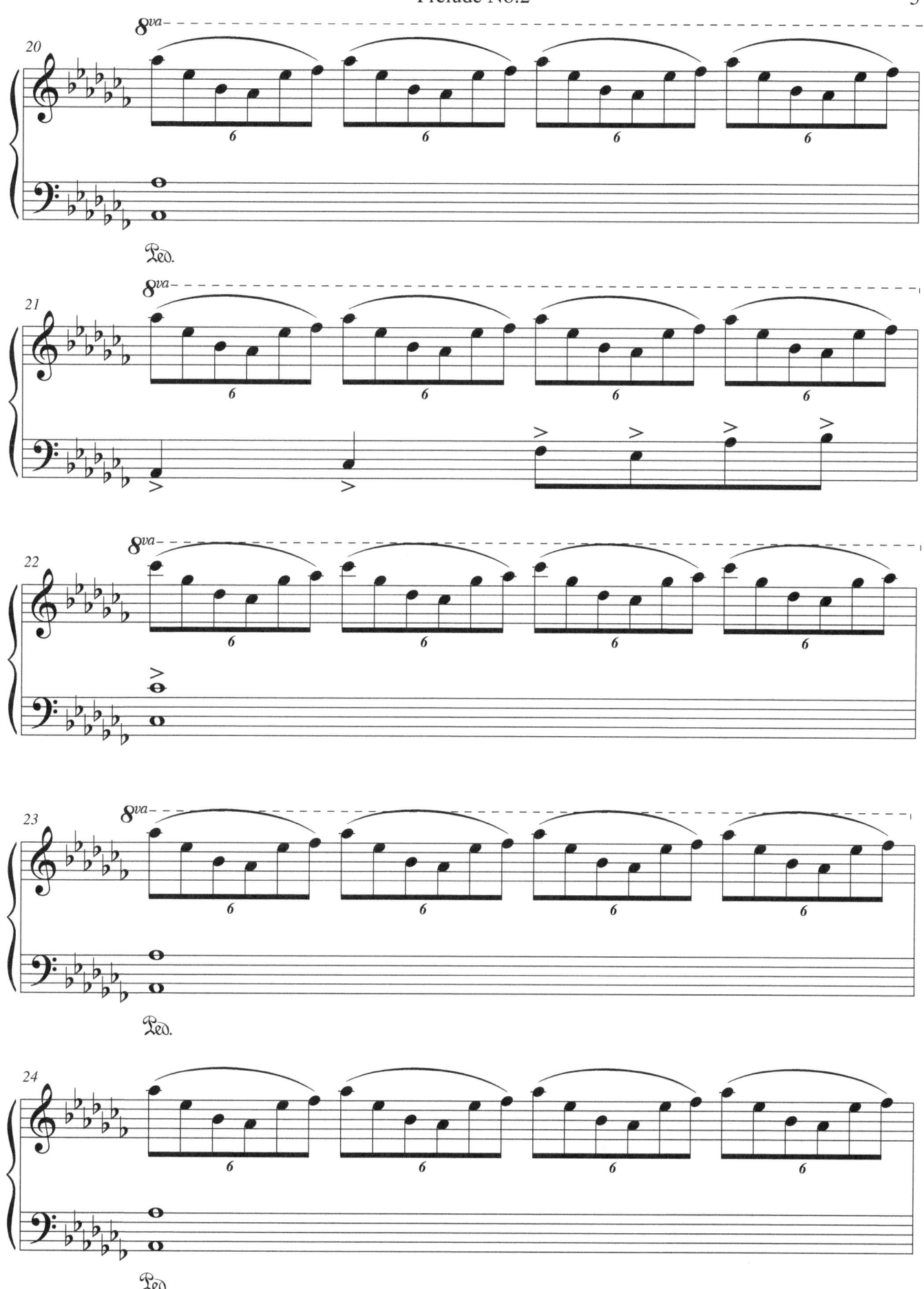

Prelude No.2

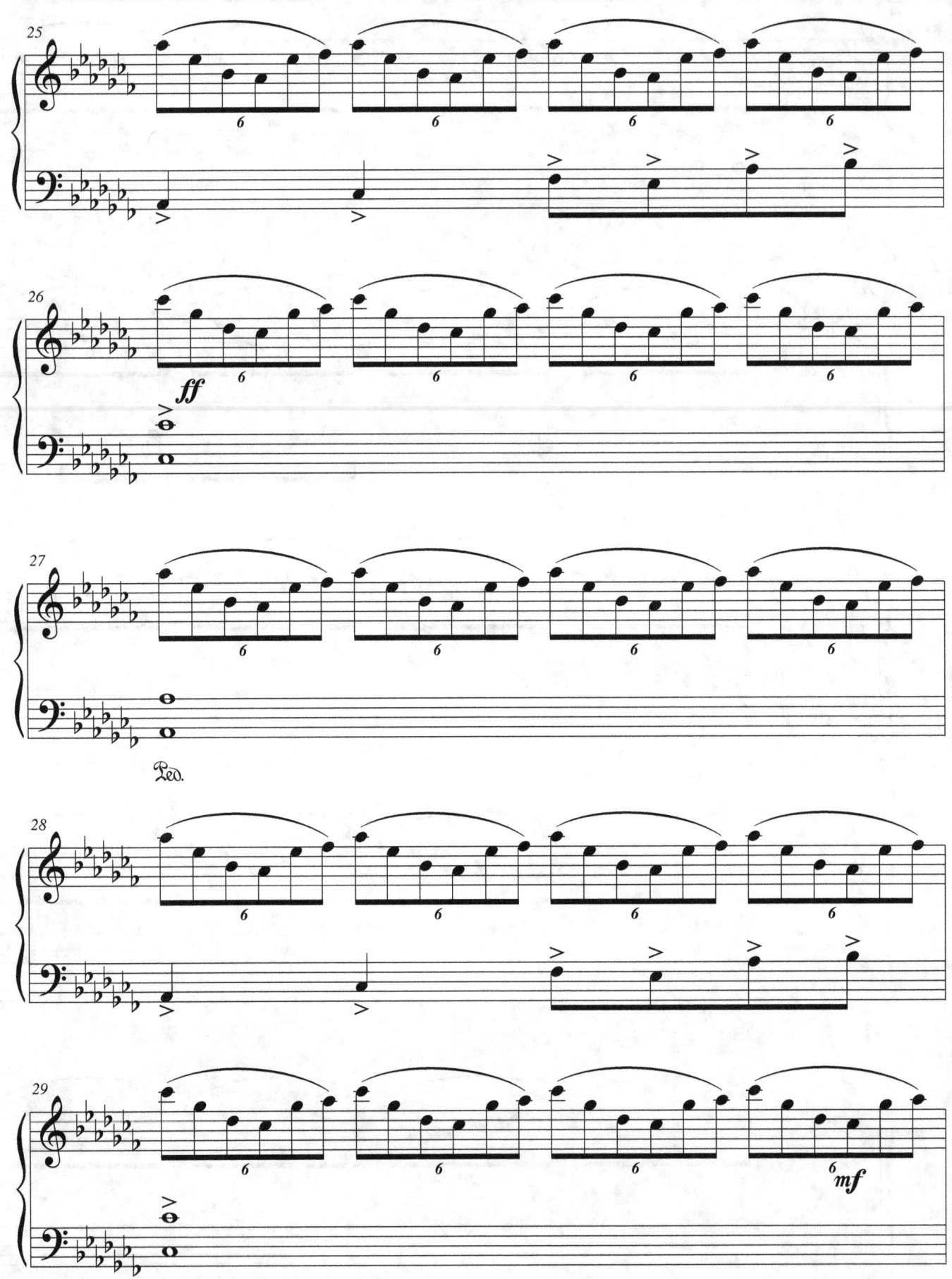

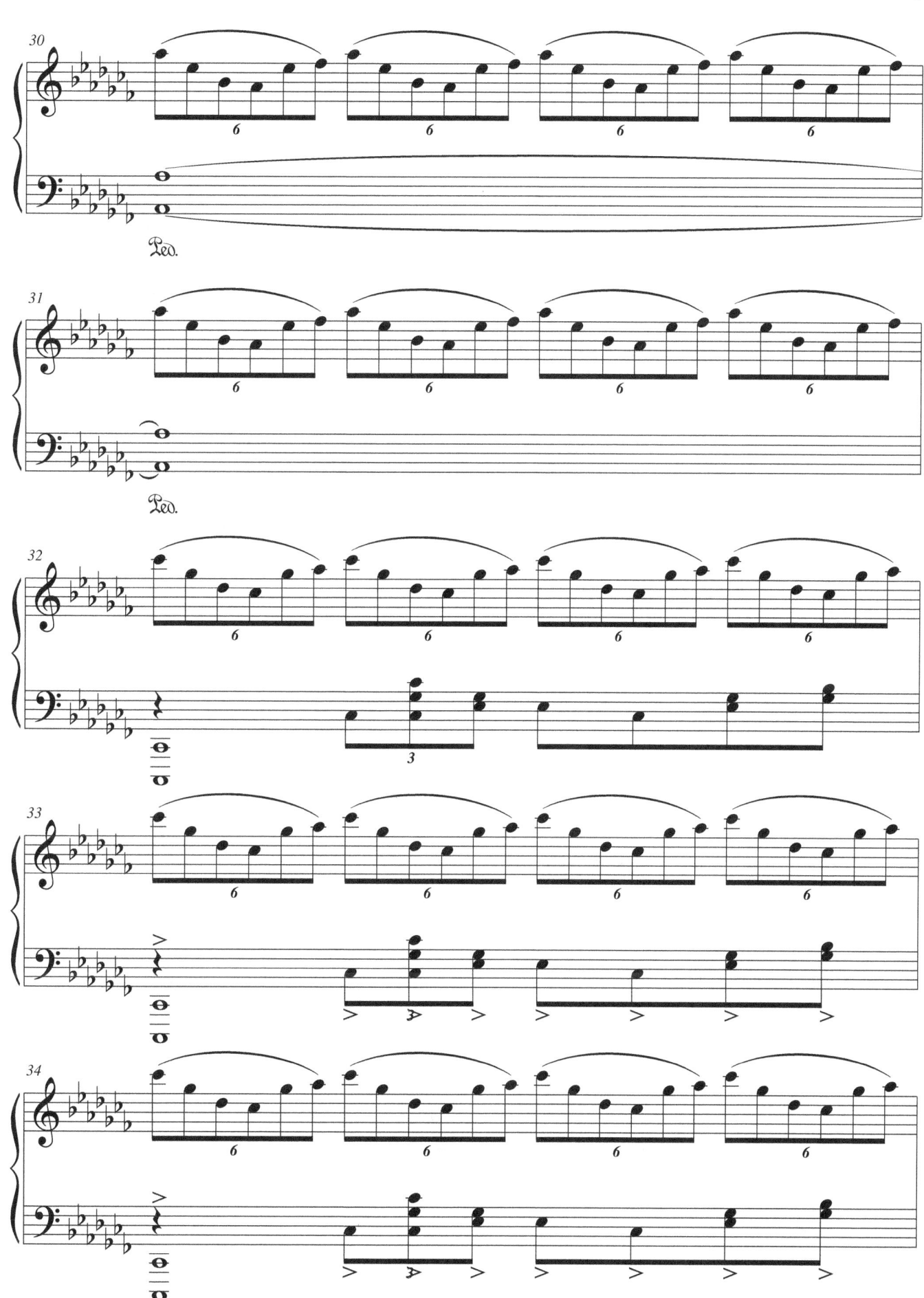

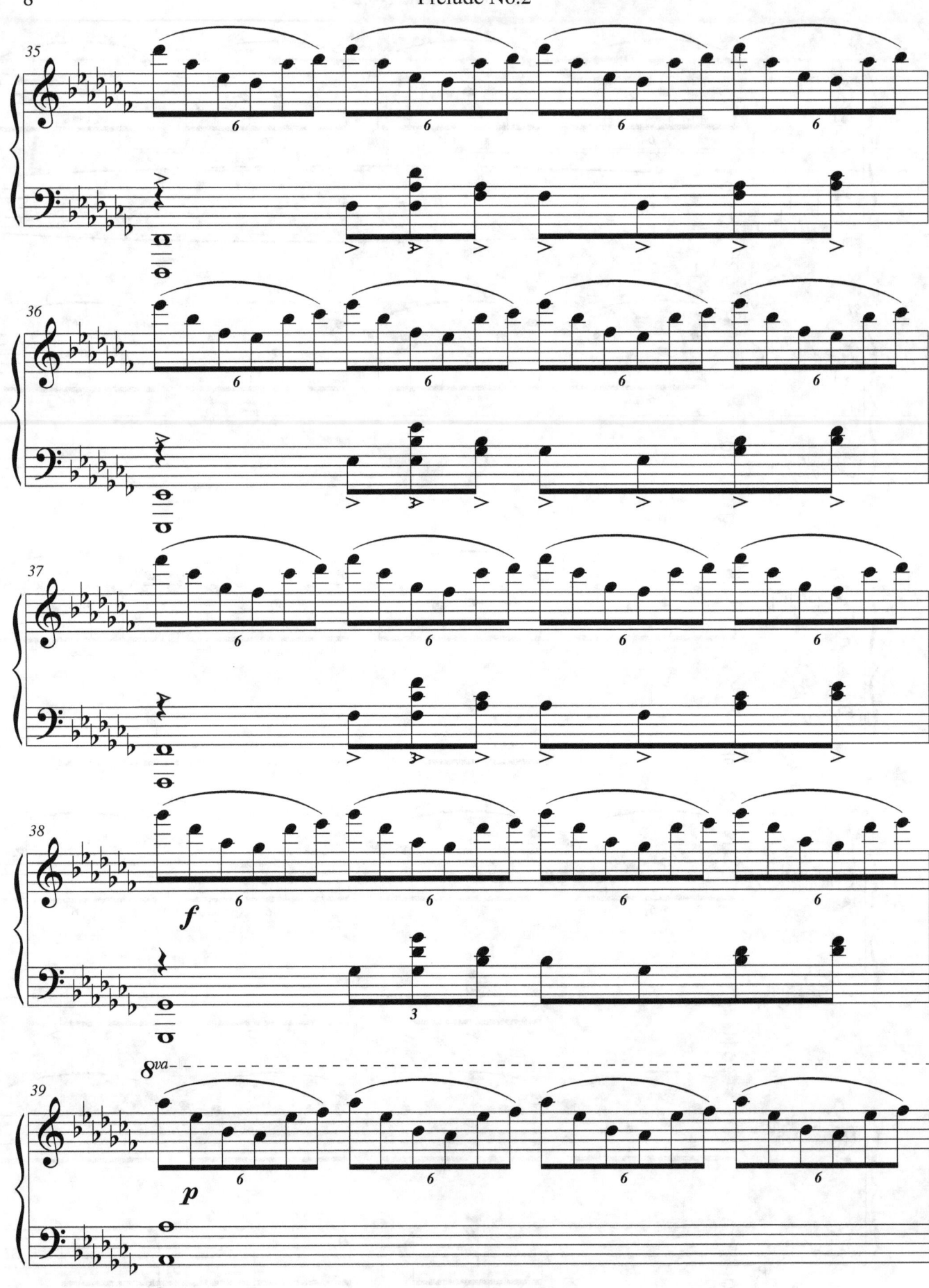

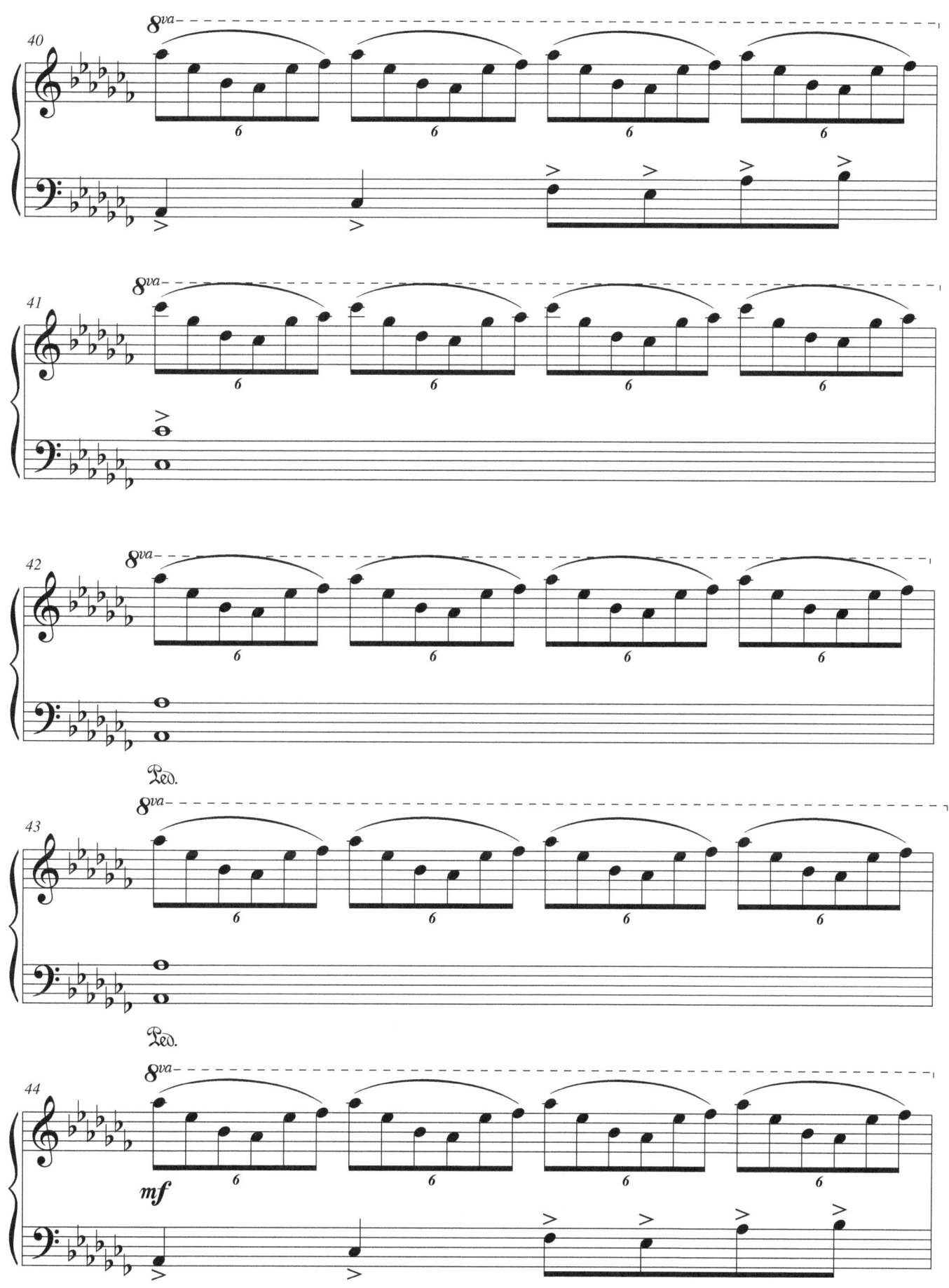

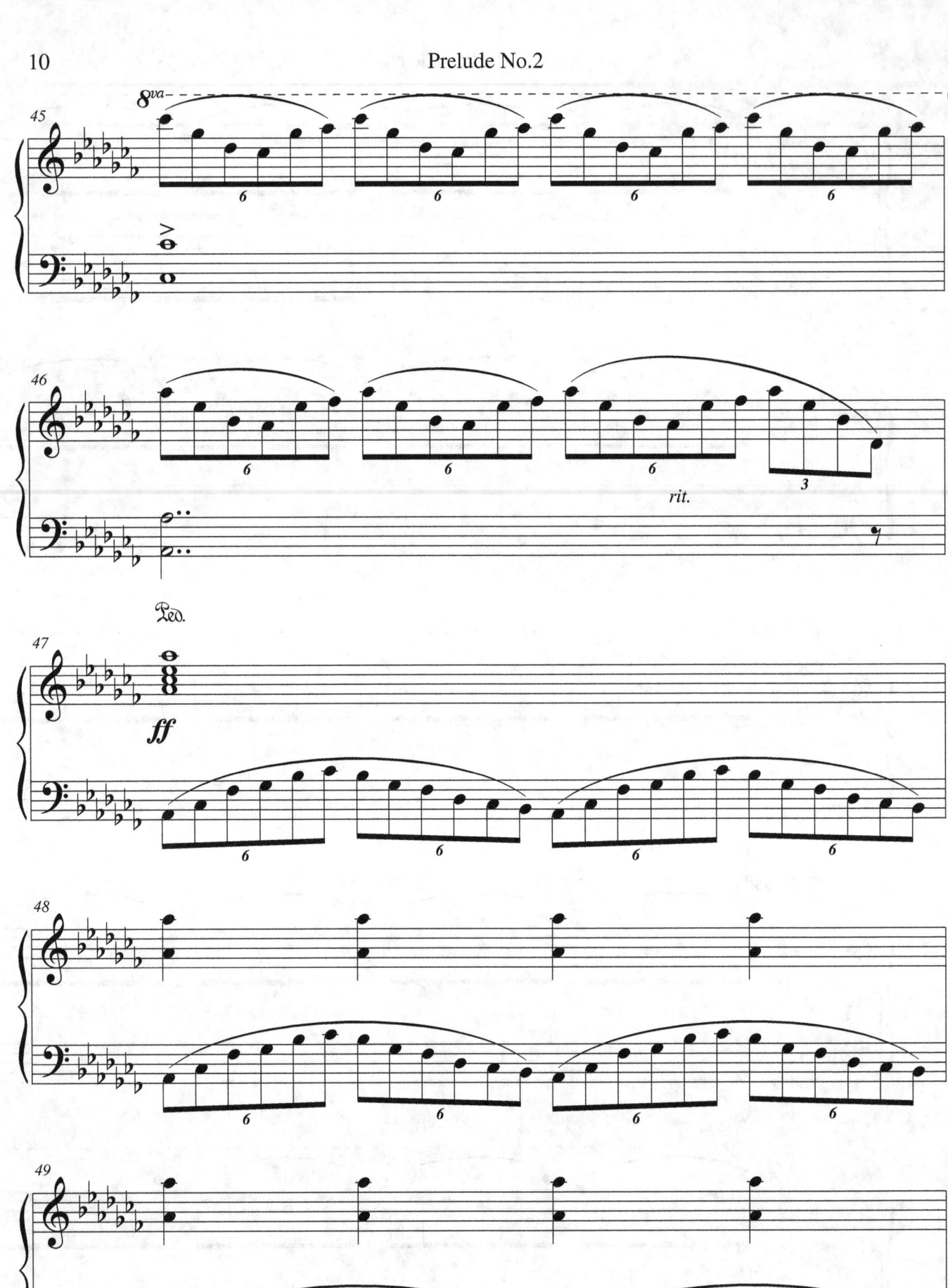

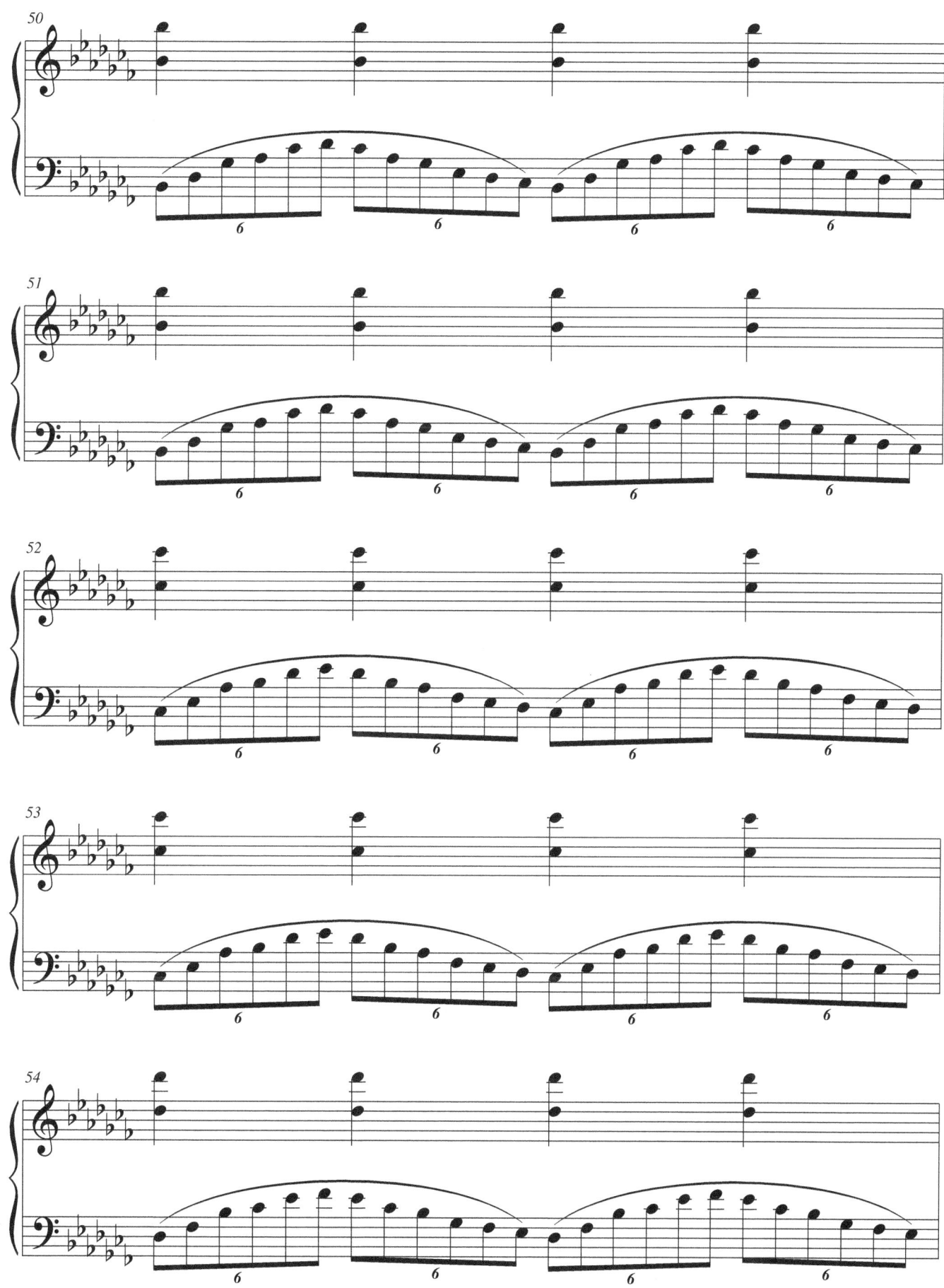

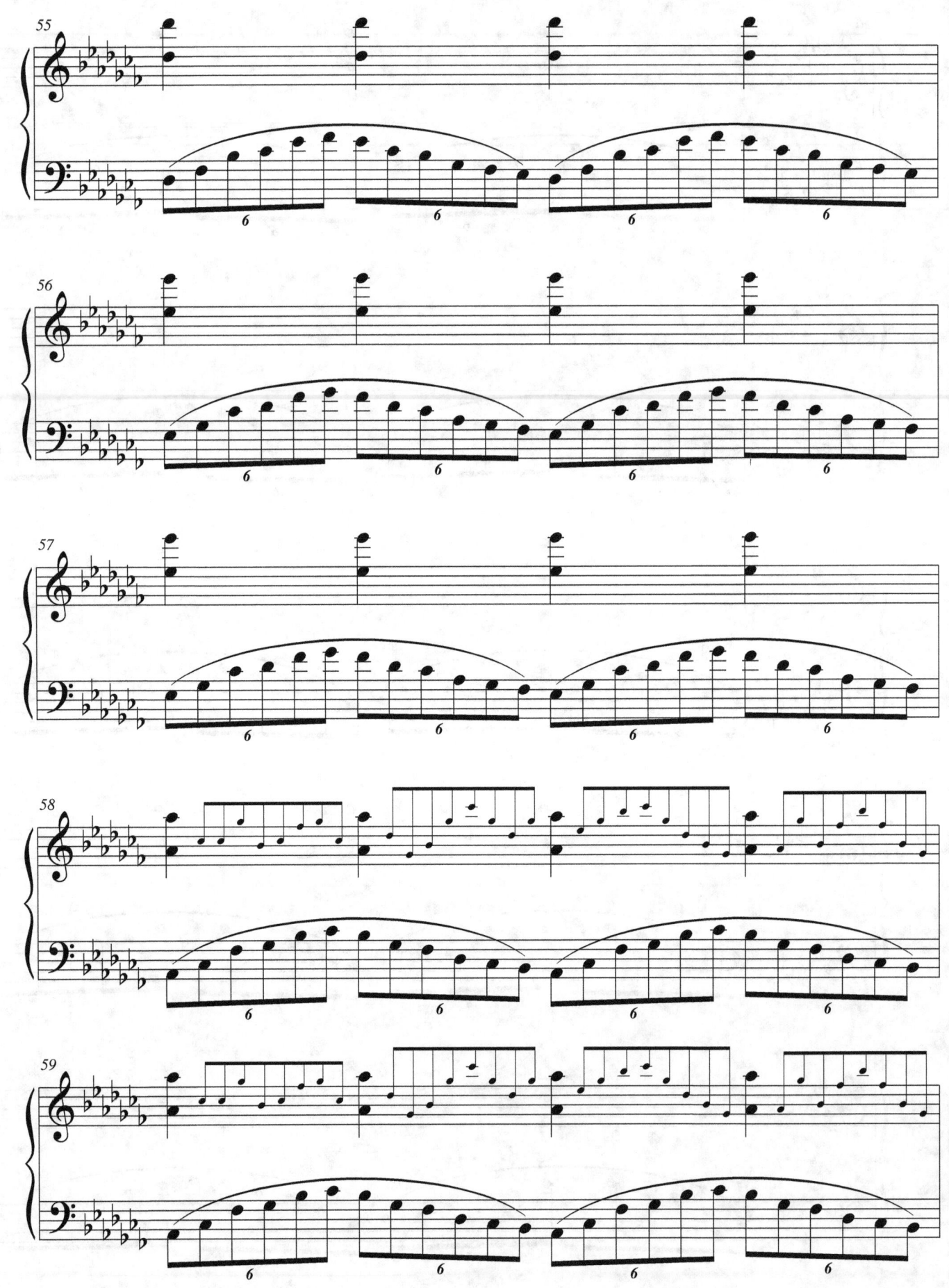

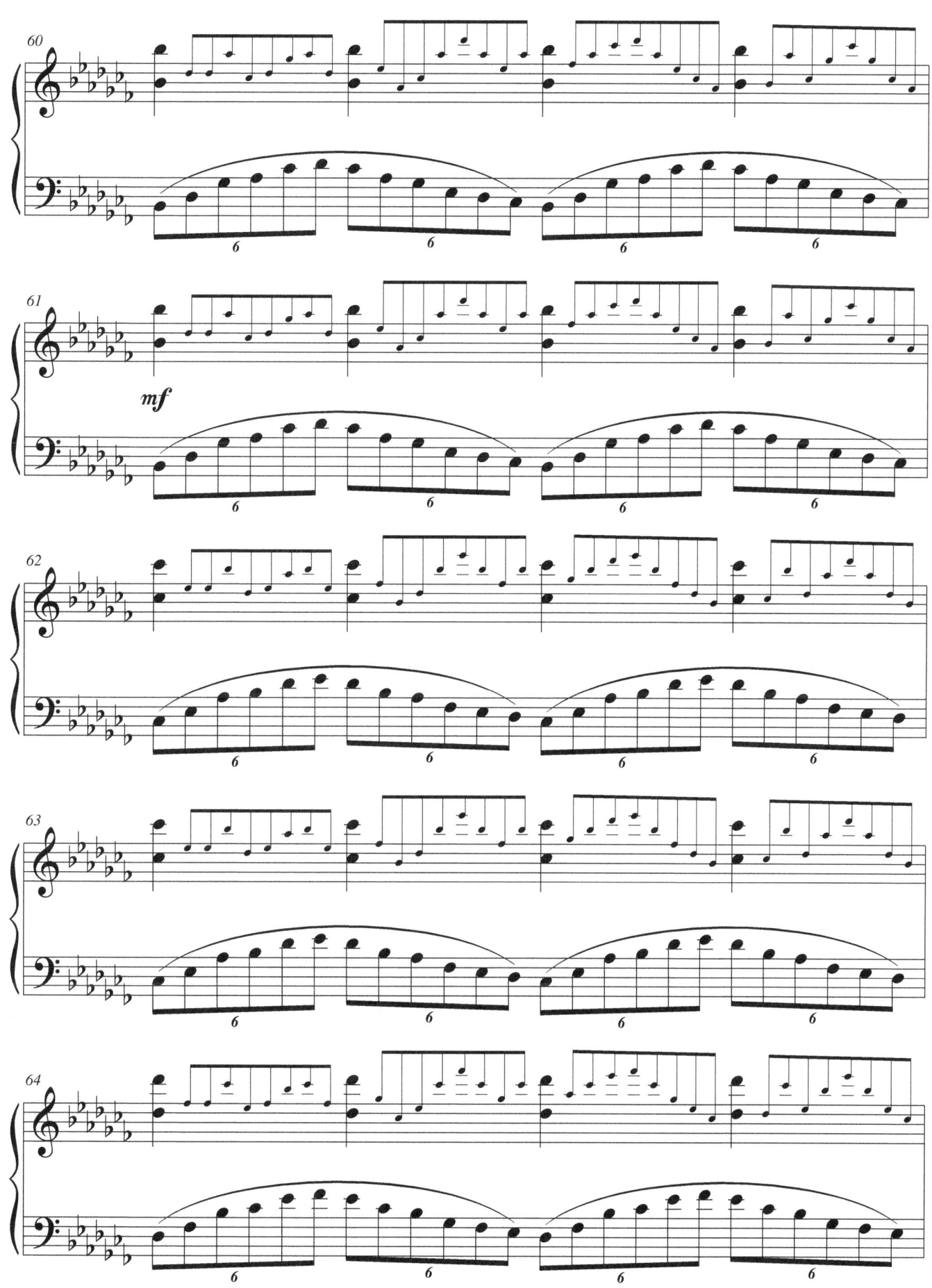

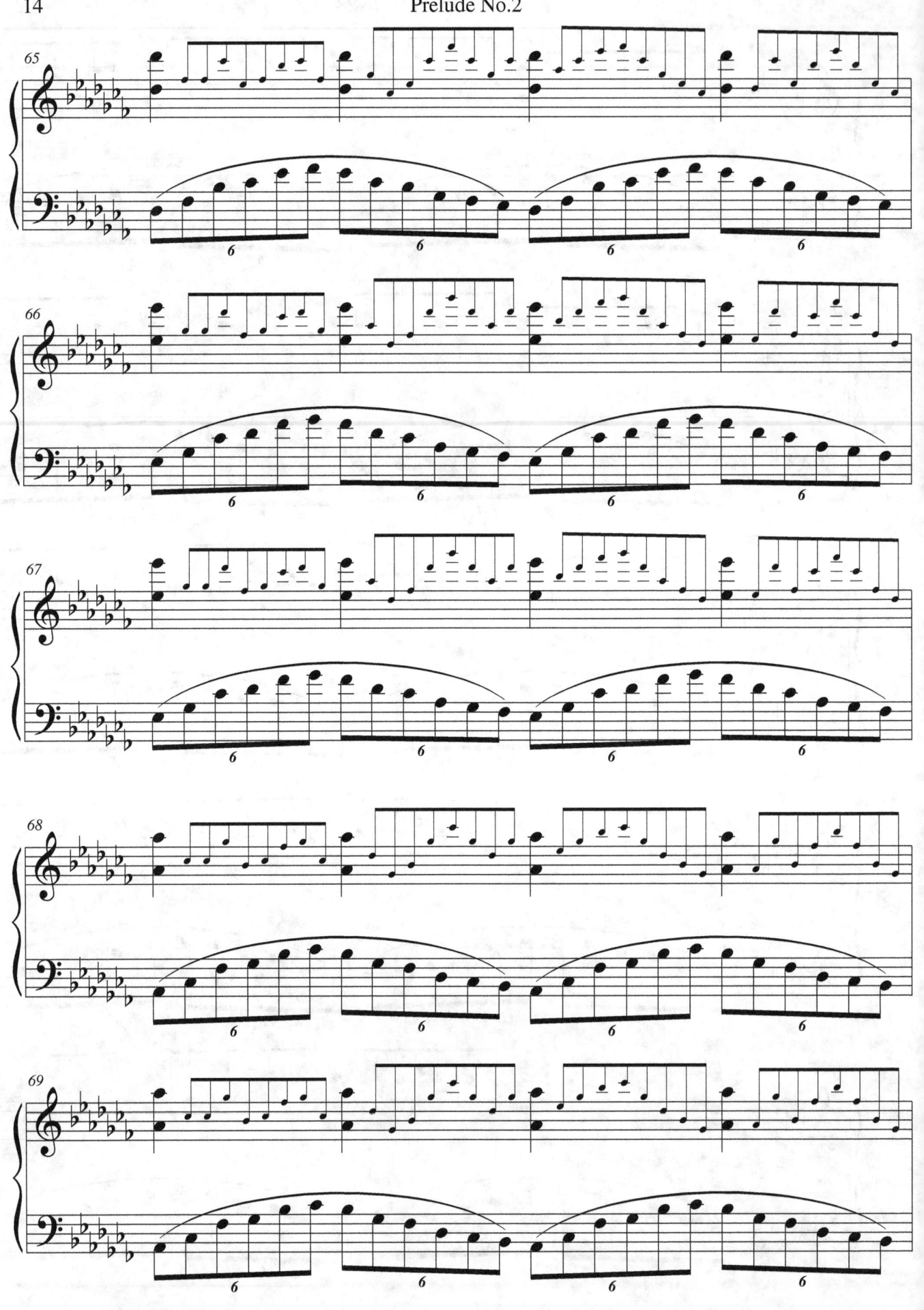

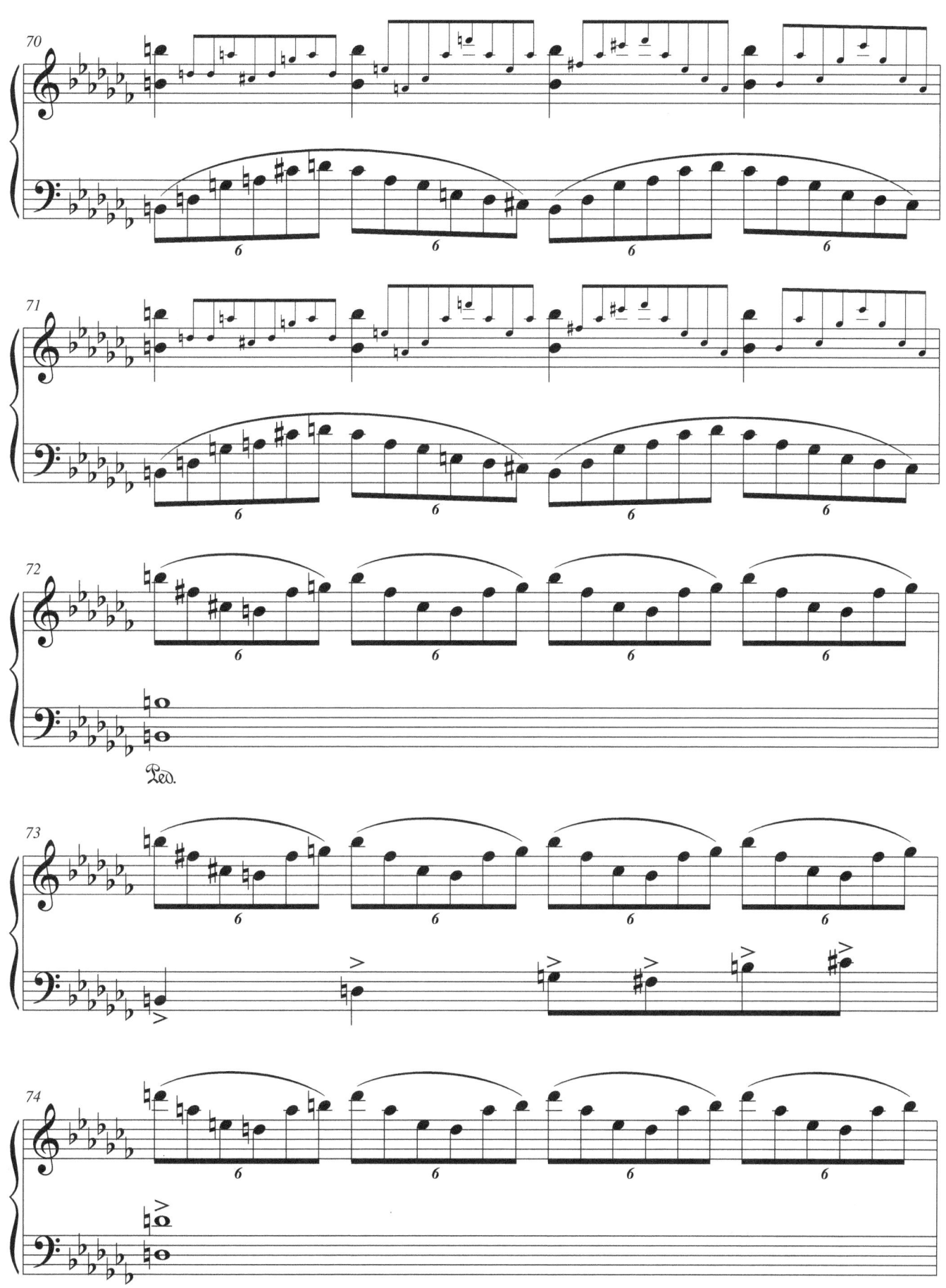

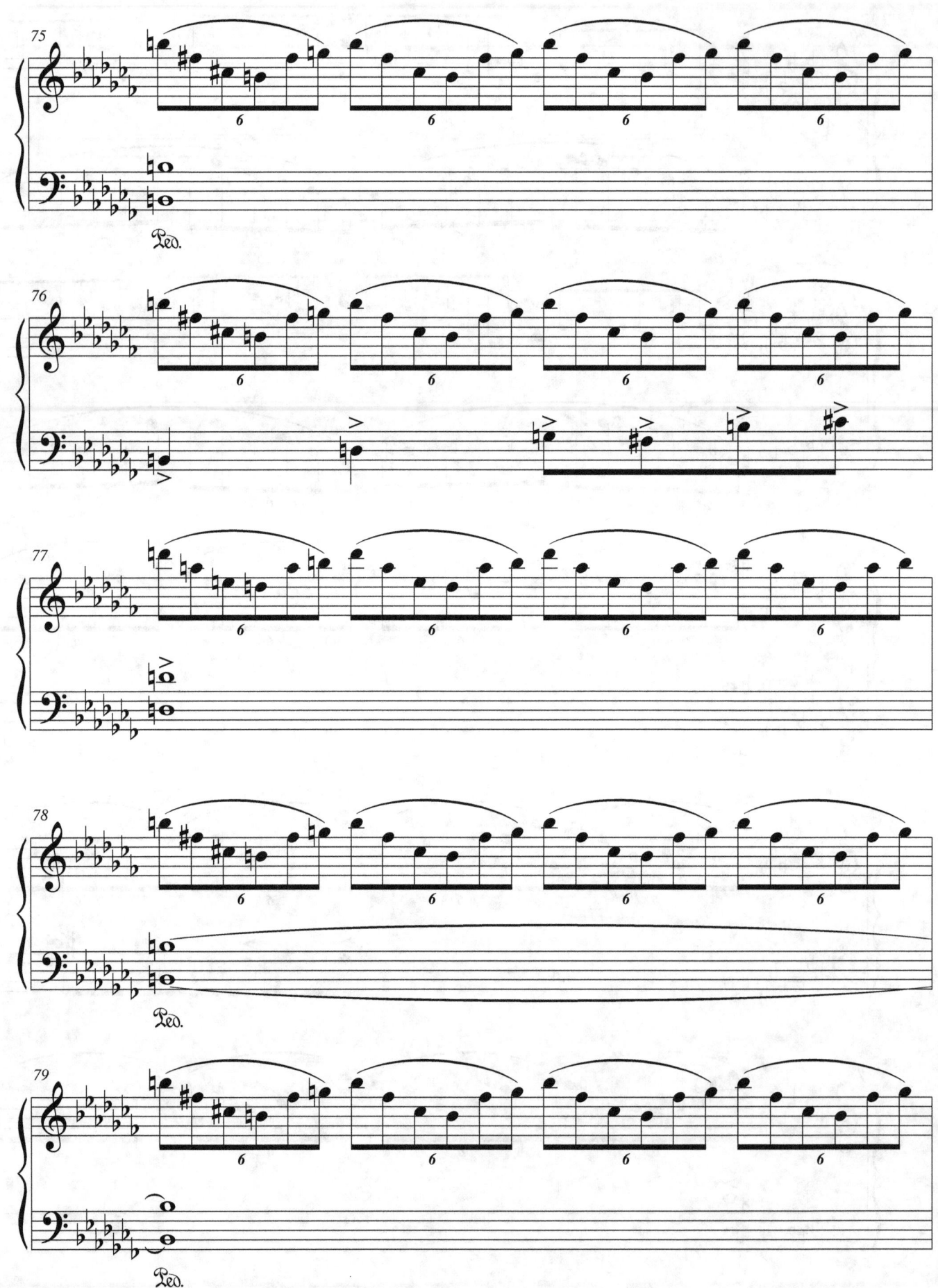

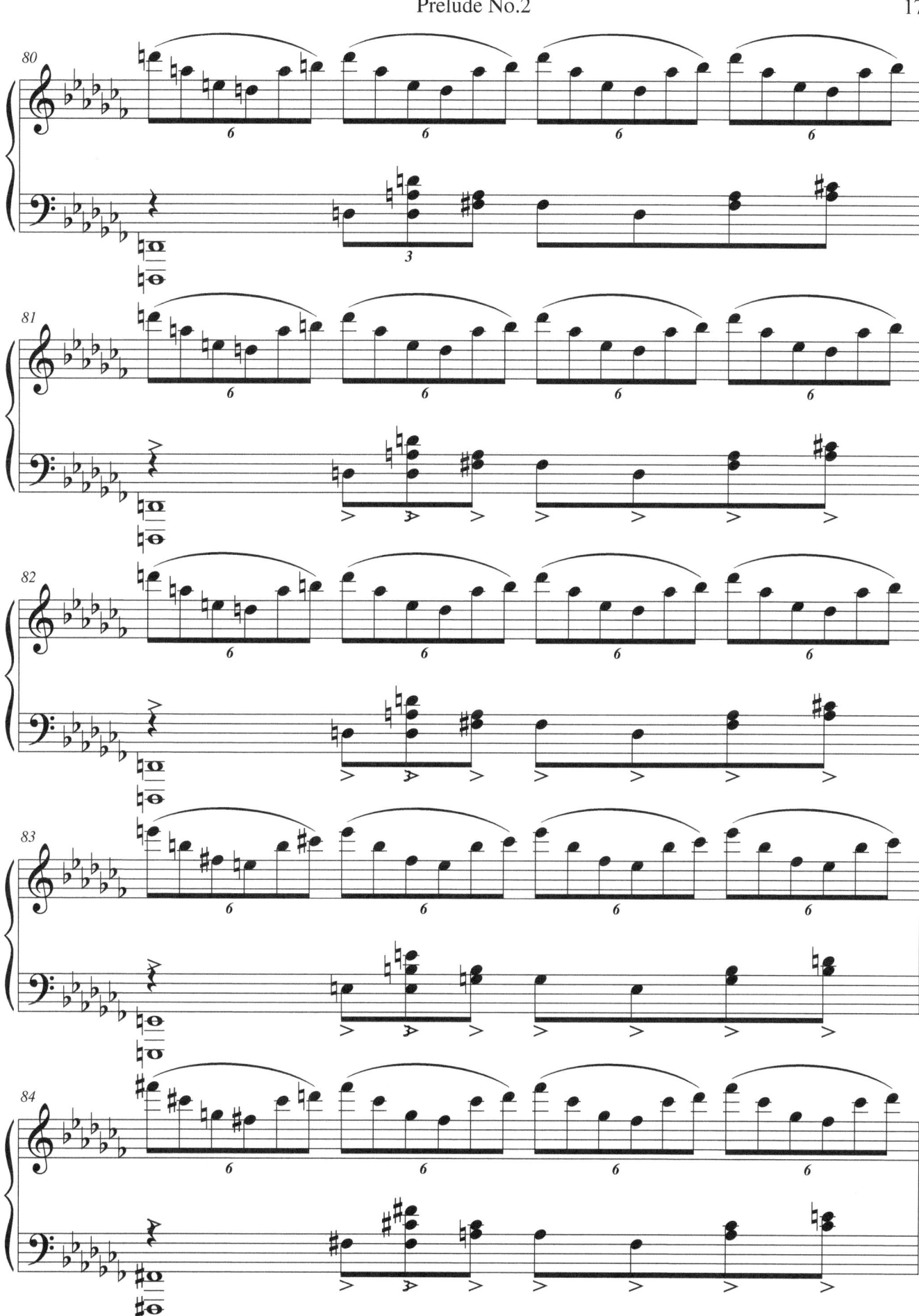

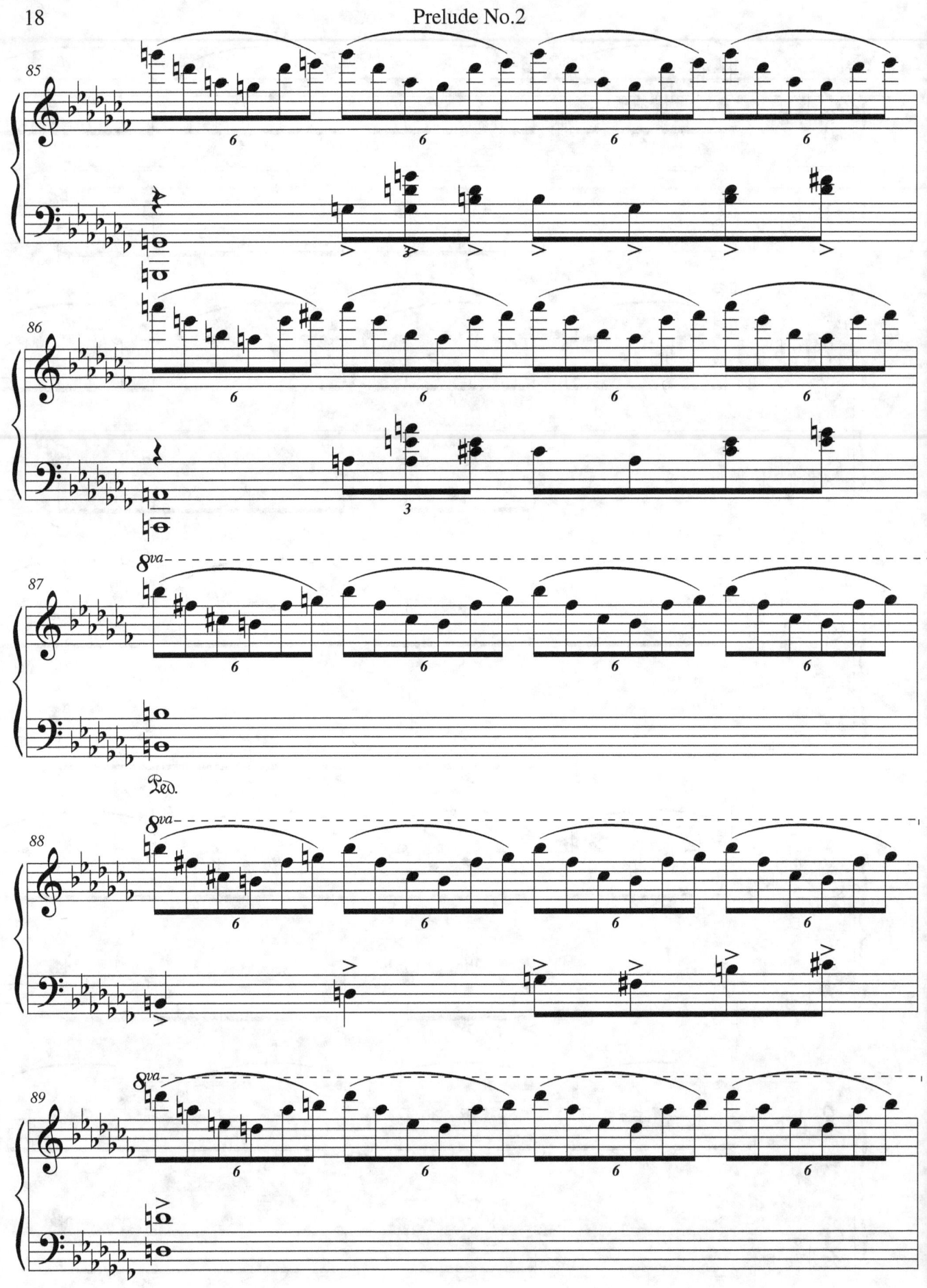

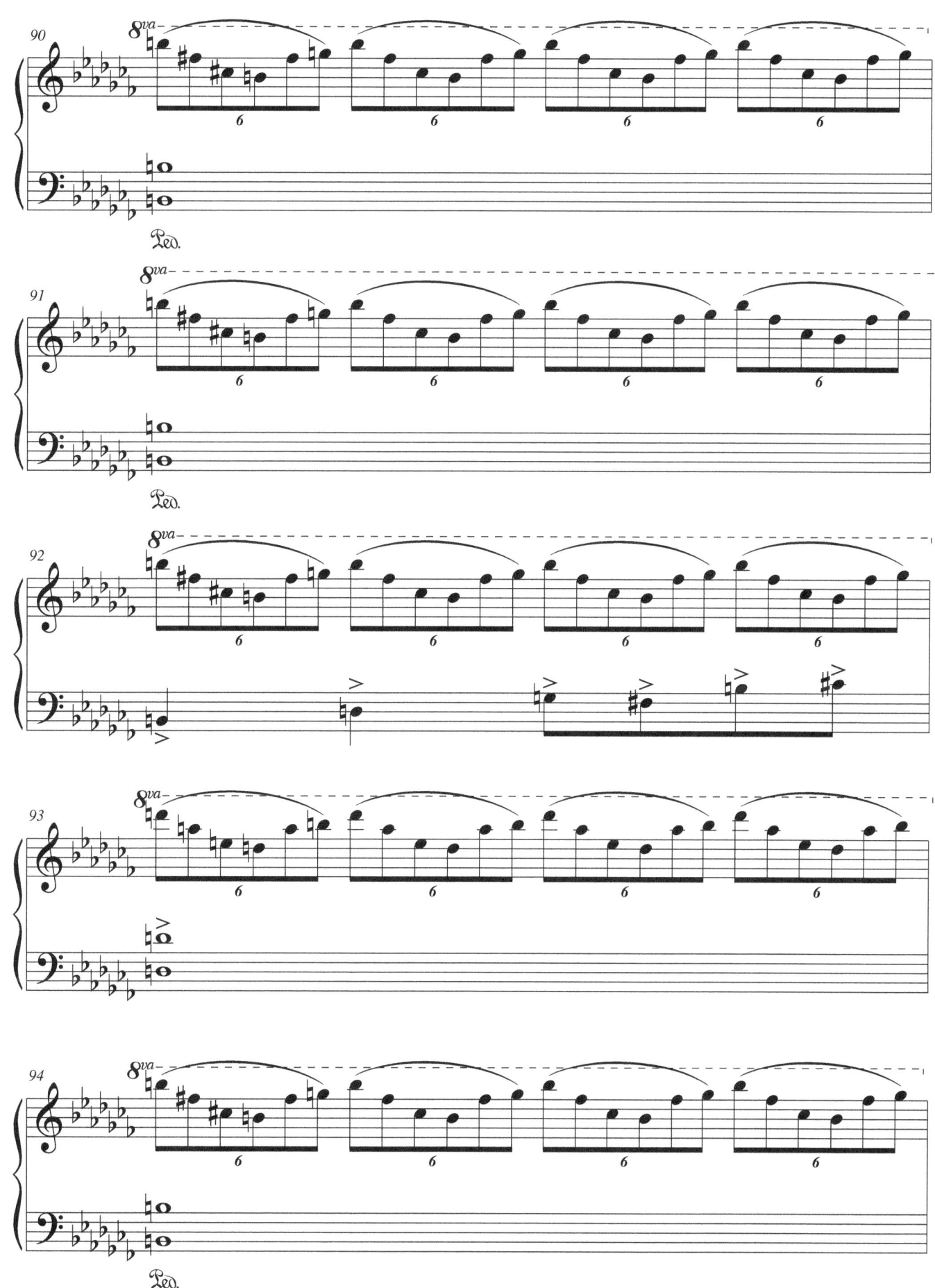

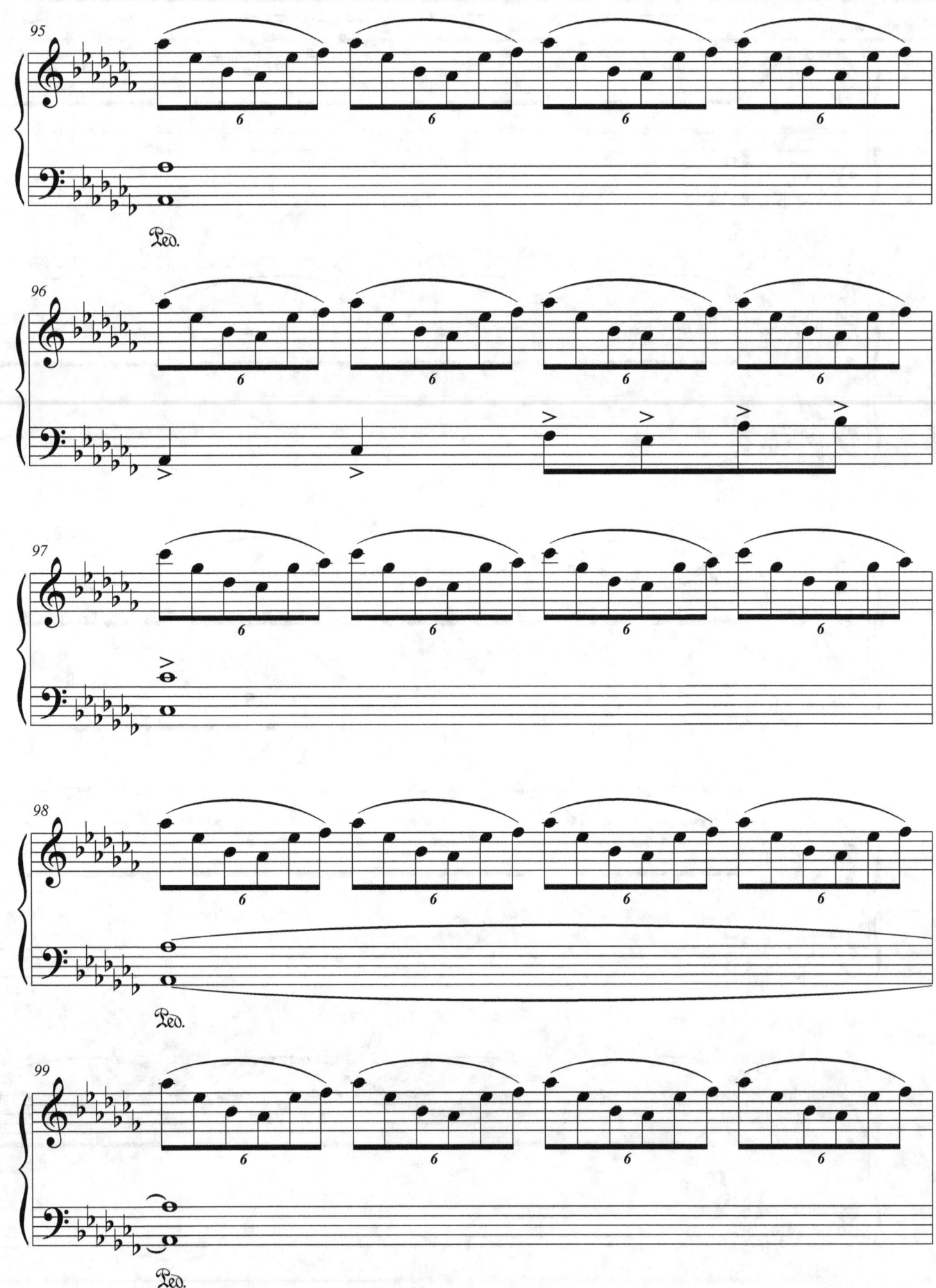

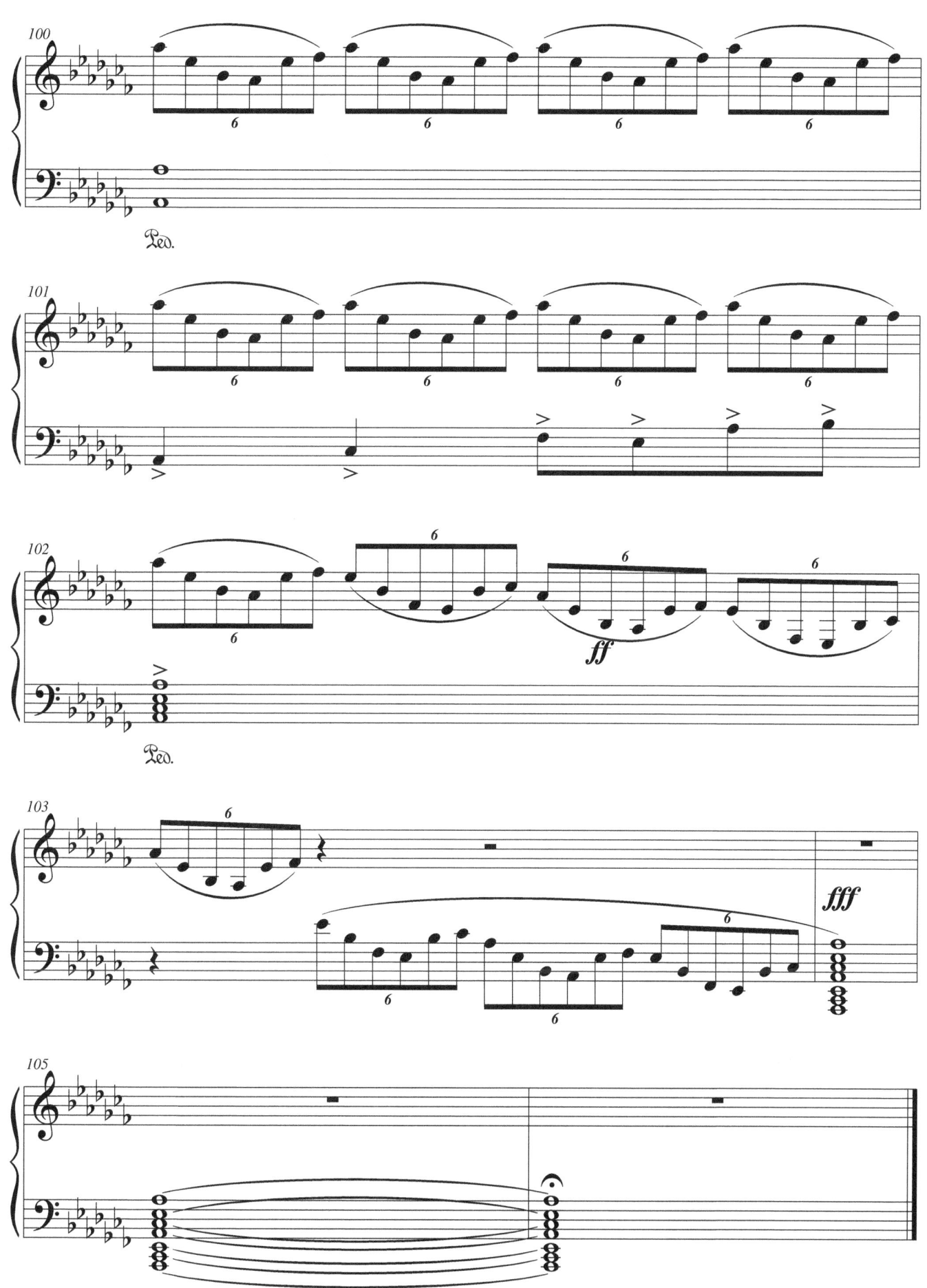

Prelude No.3

Dubiell De Zarraga Lago

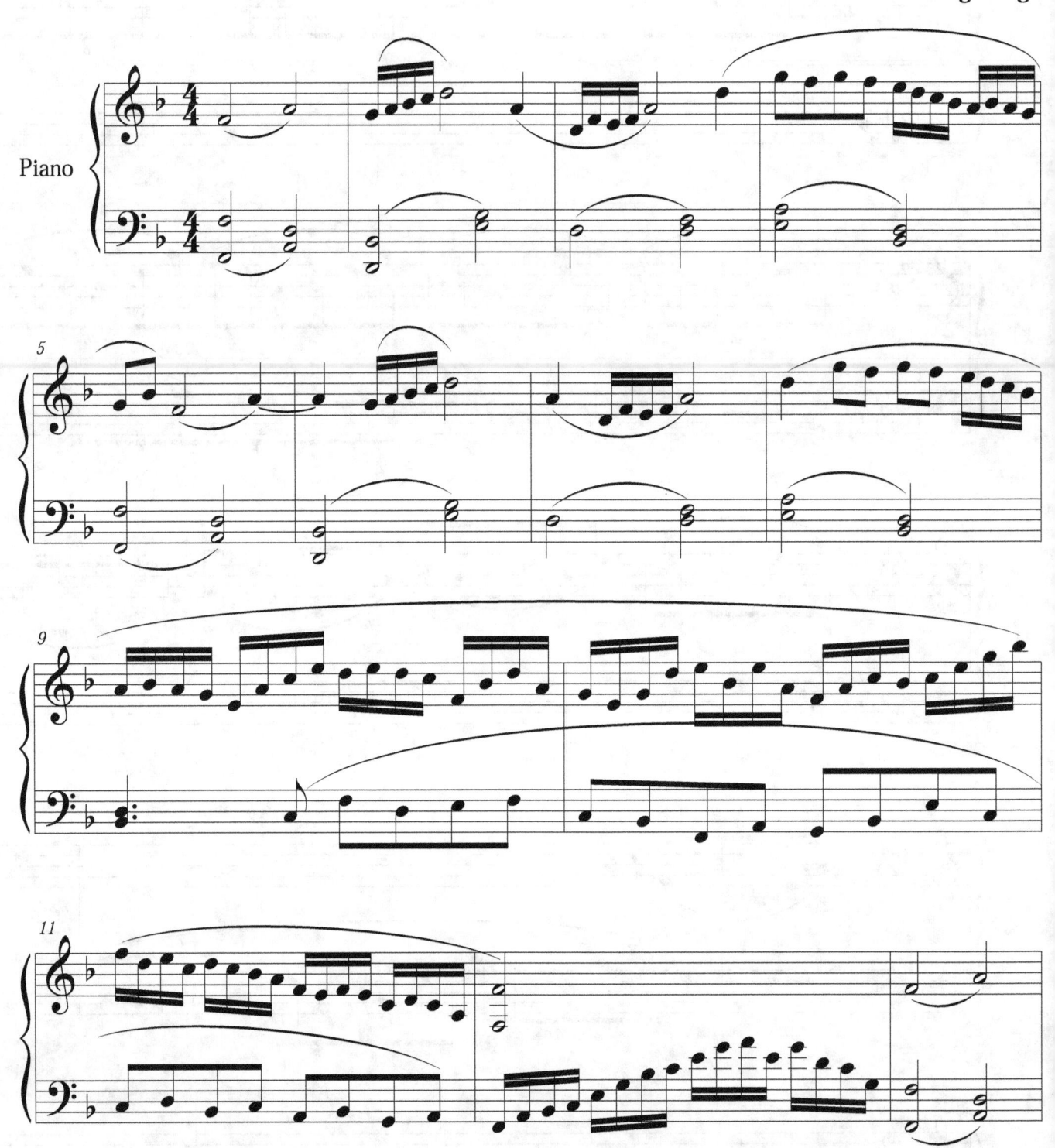

Prelude No.3

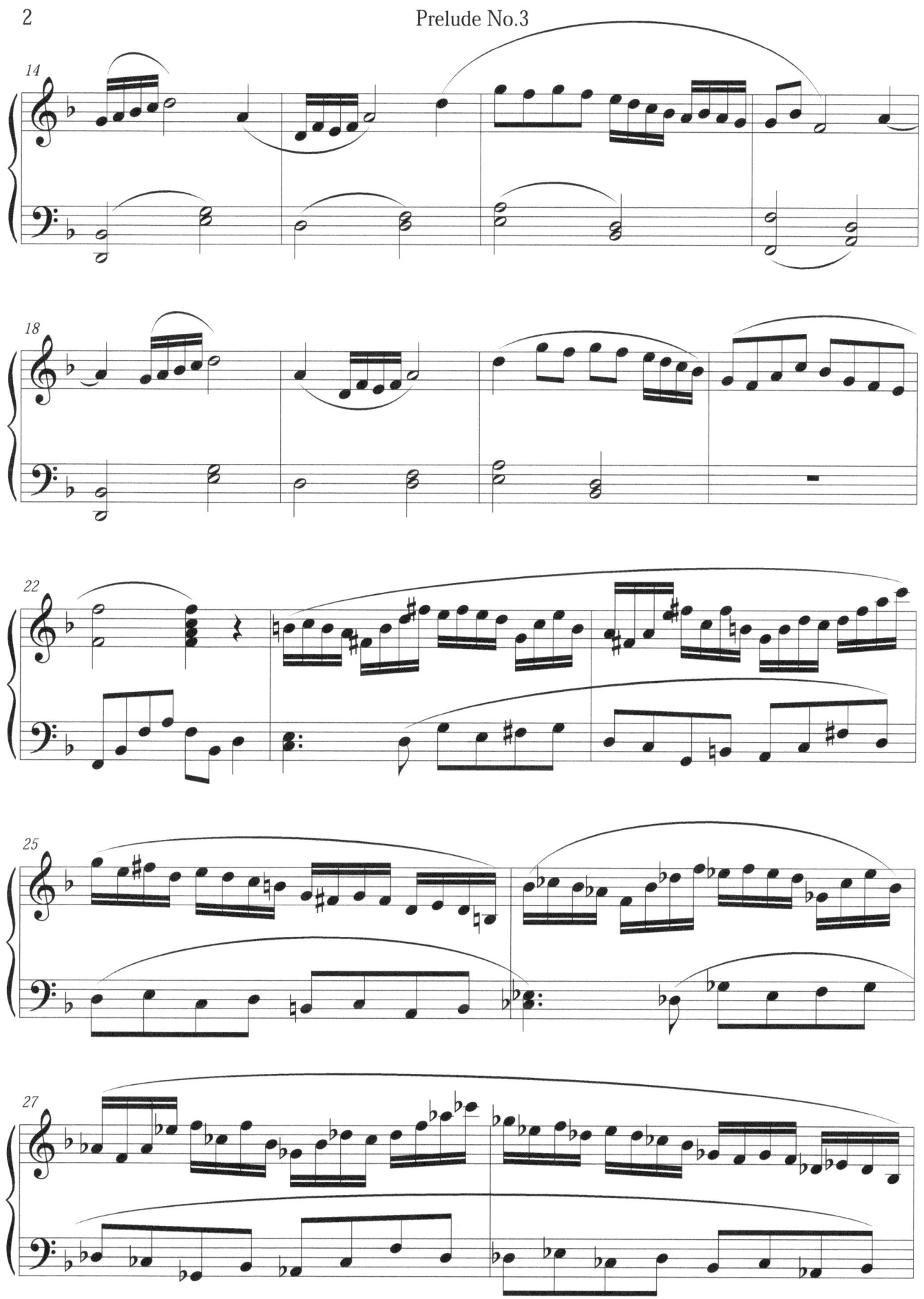

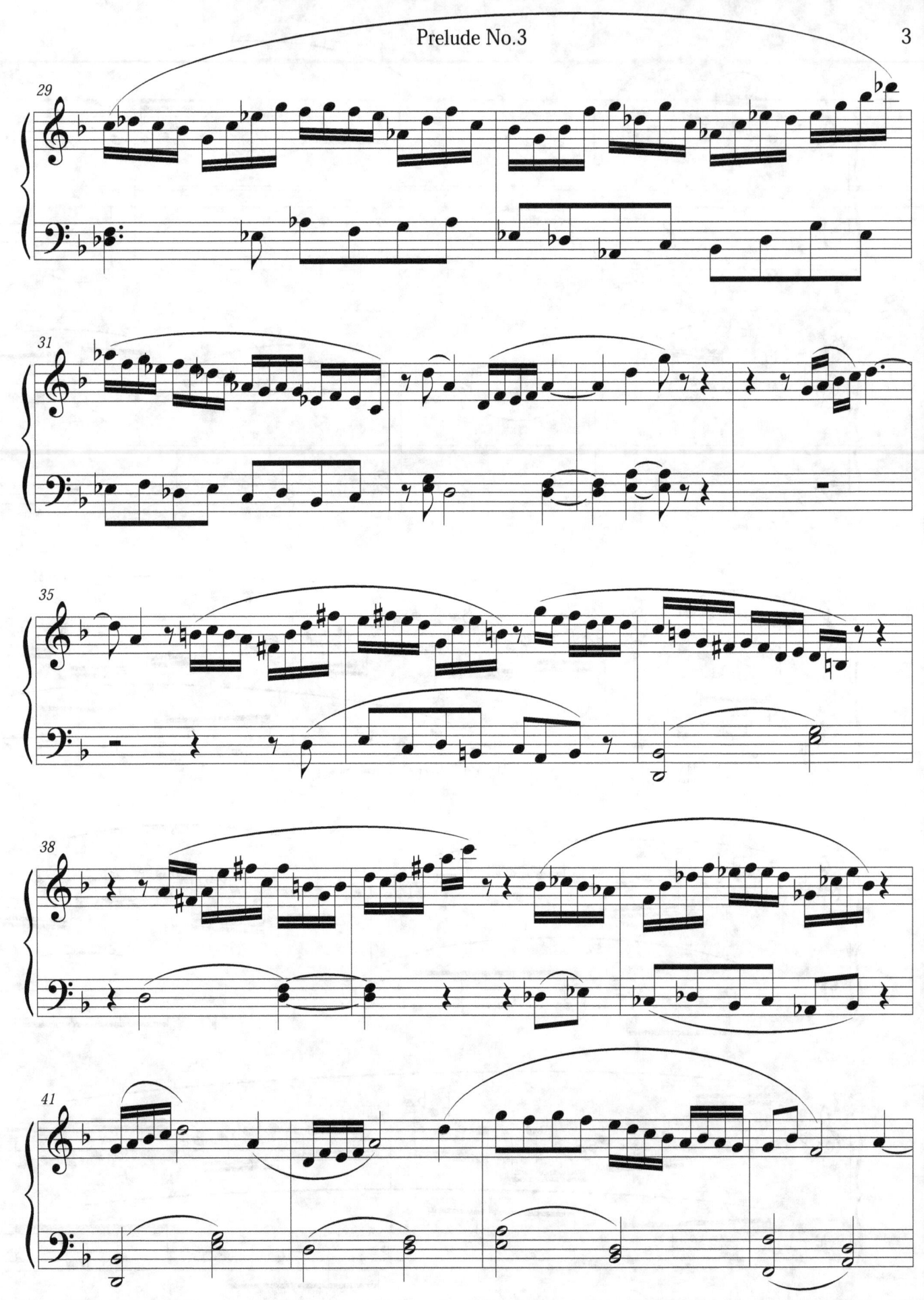

Prelude No.3

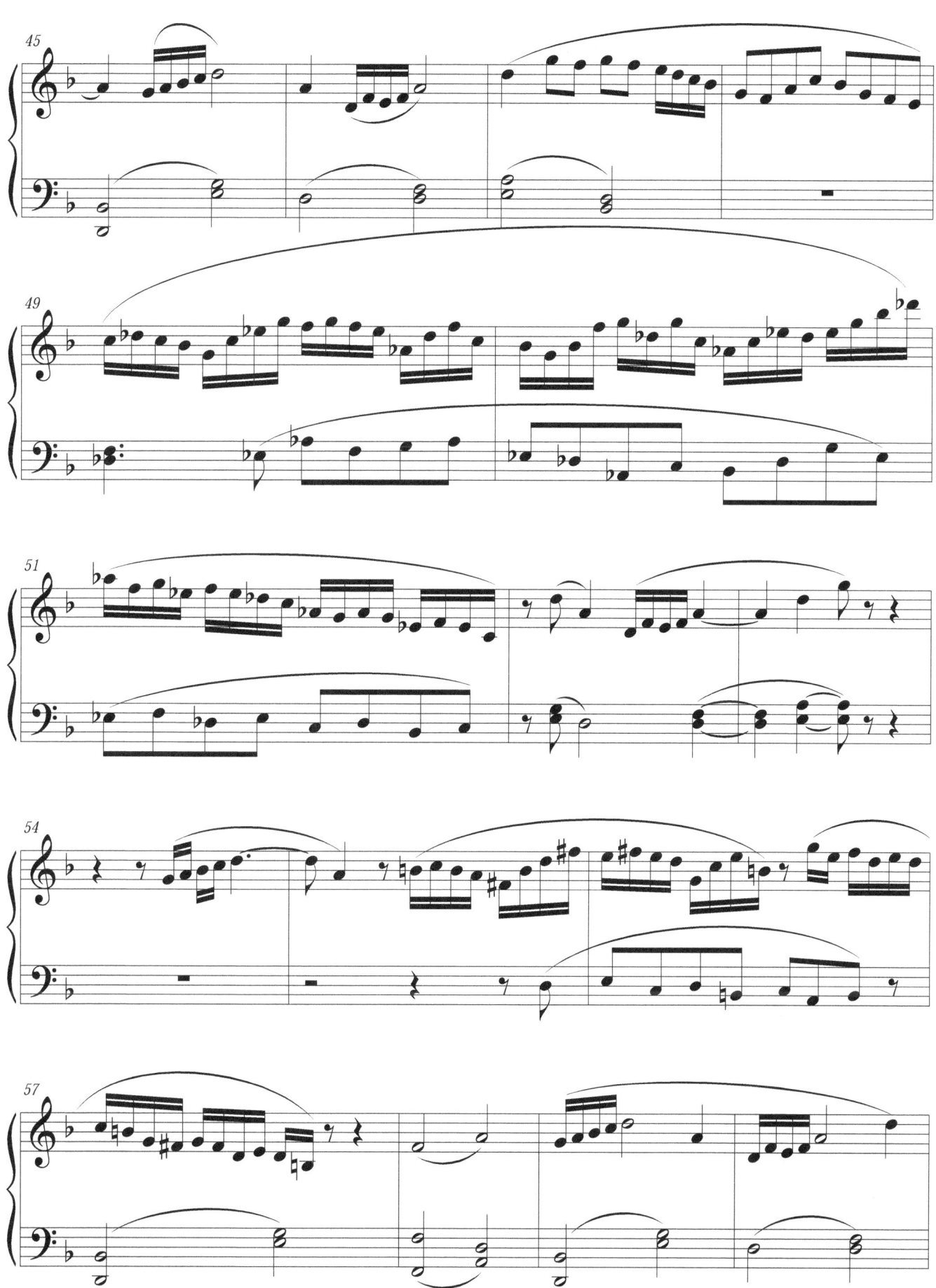

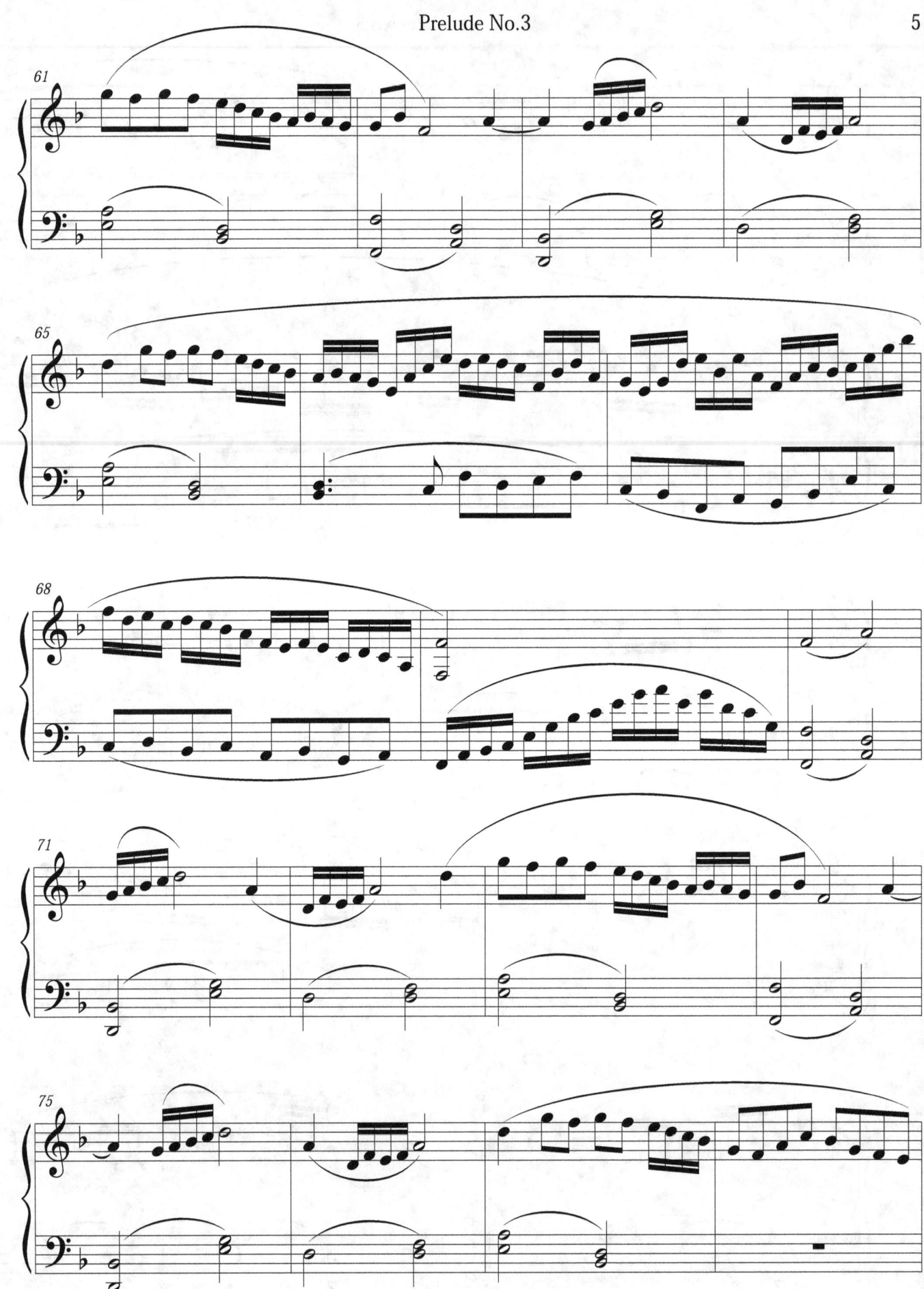

Prelude No.3

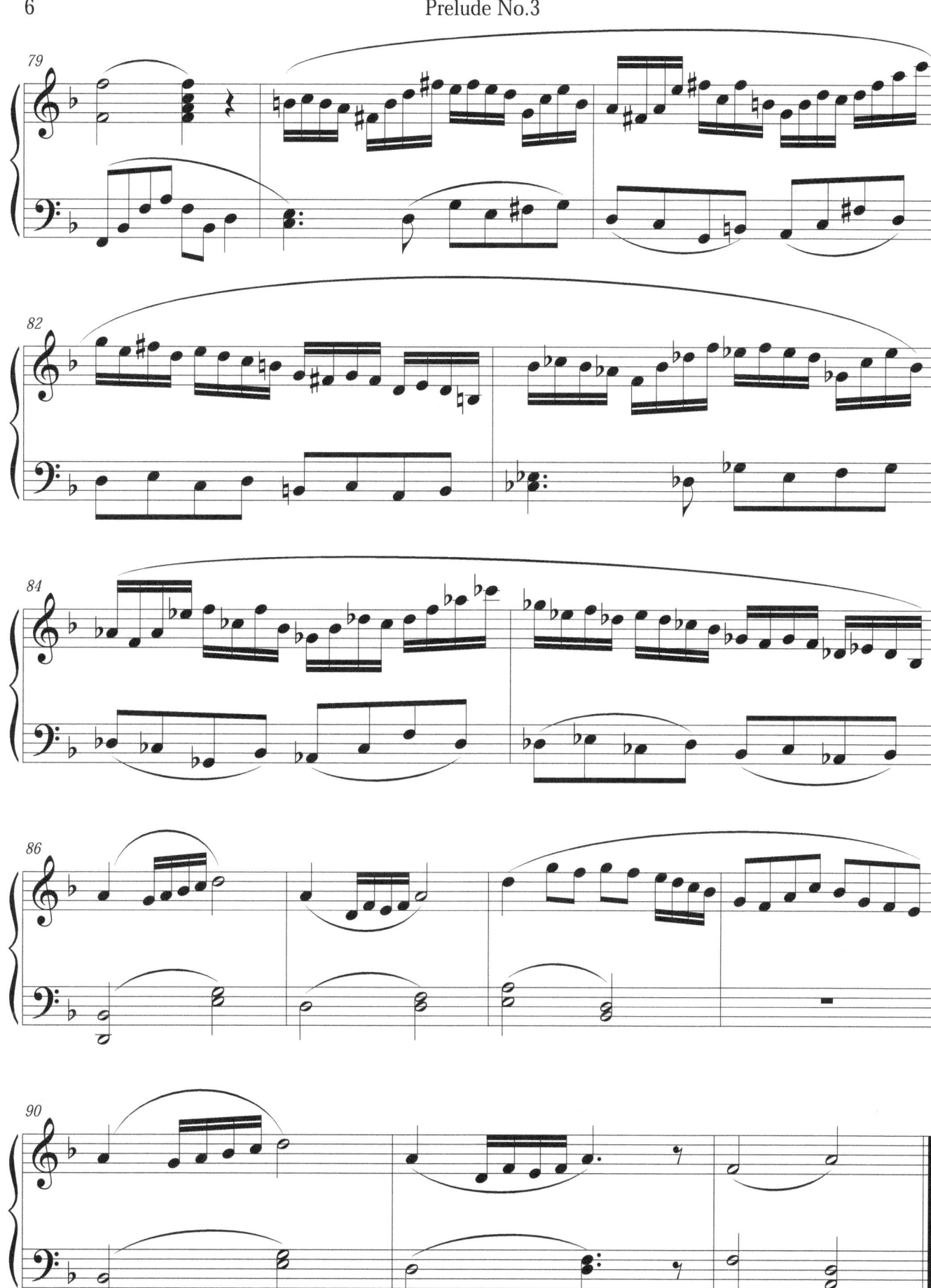

Prelude No.4

Dubiell A De Zarraga Lago

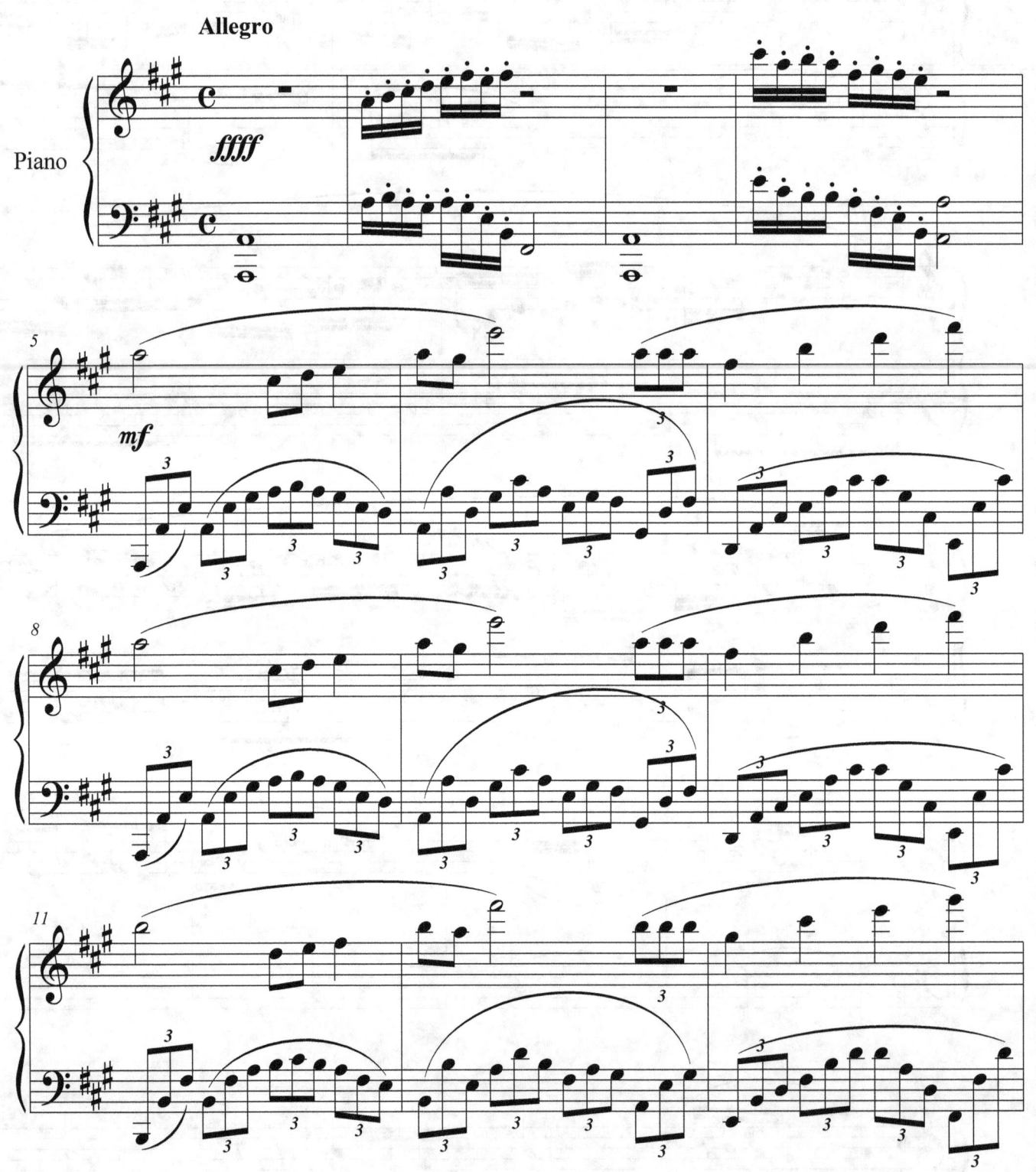

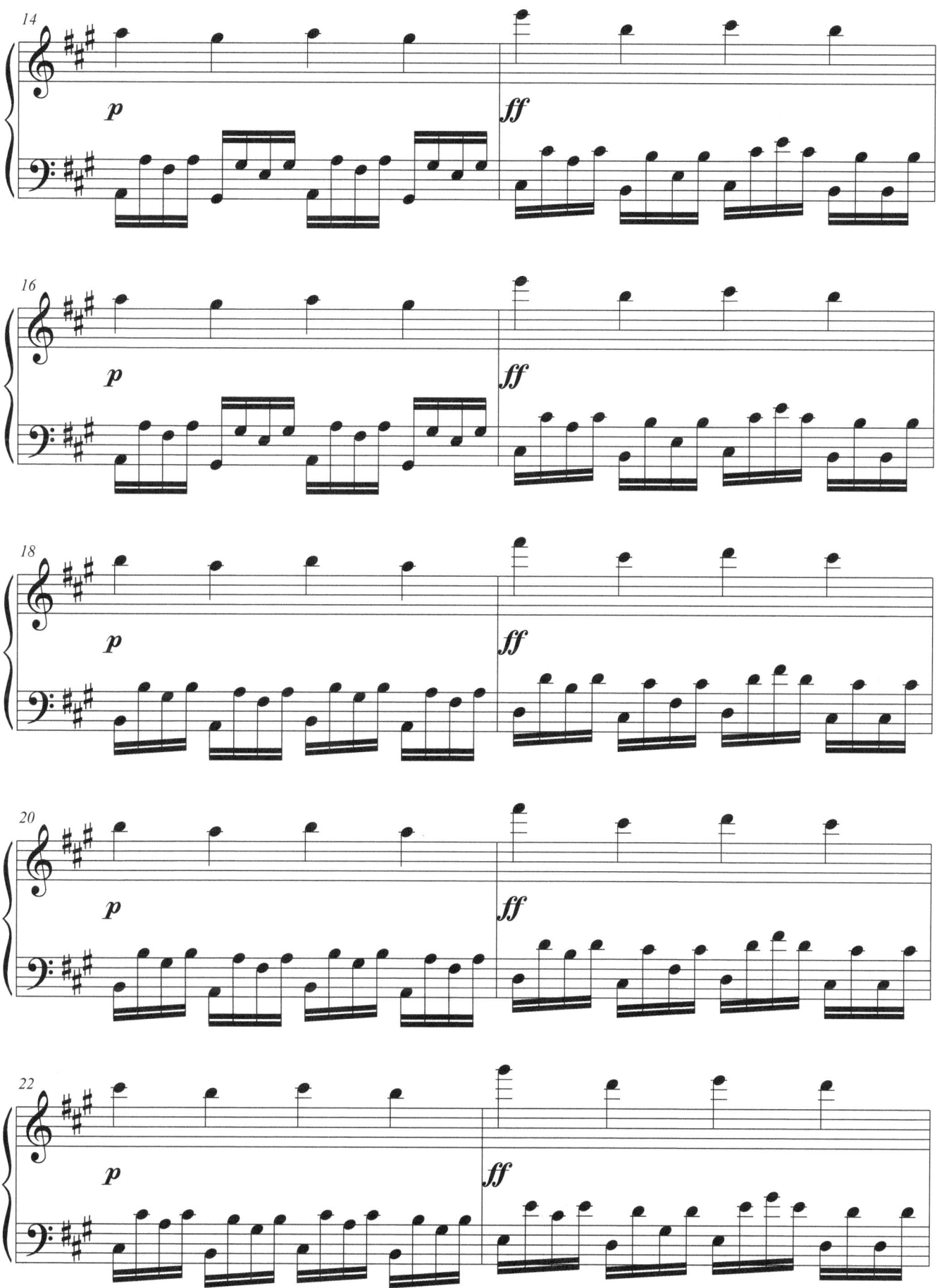

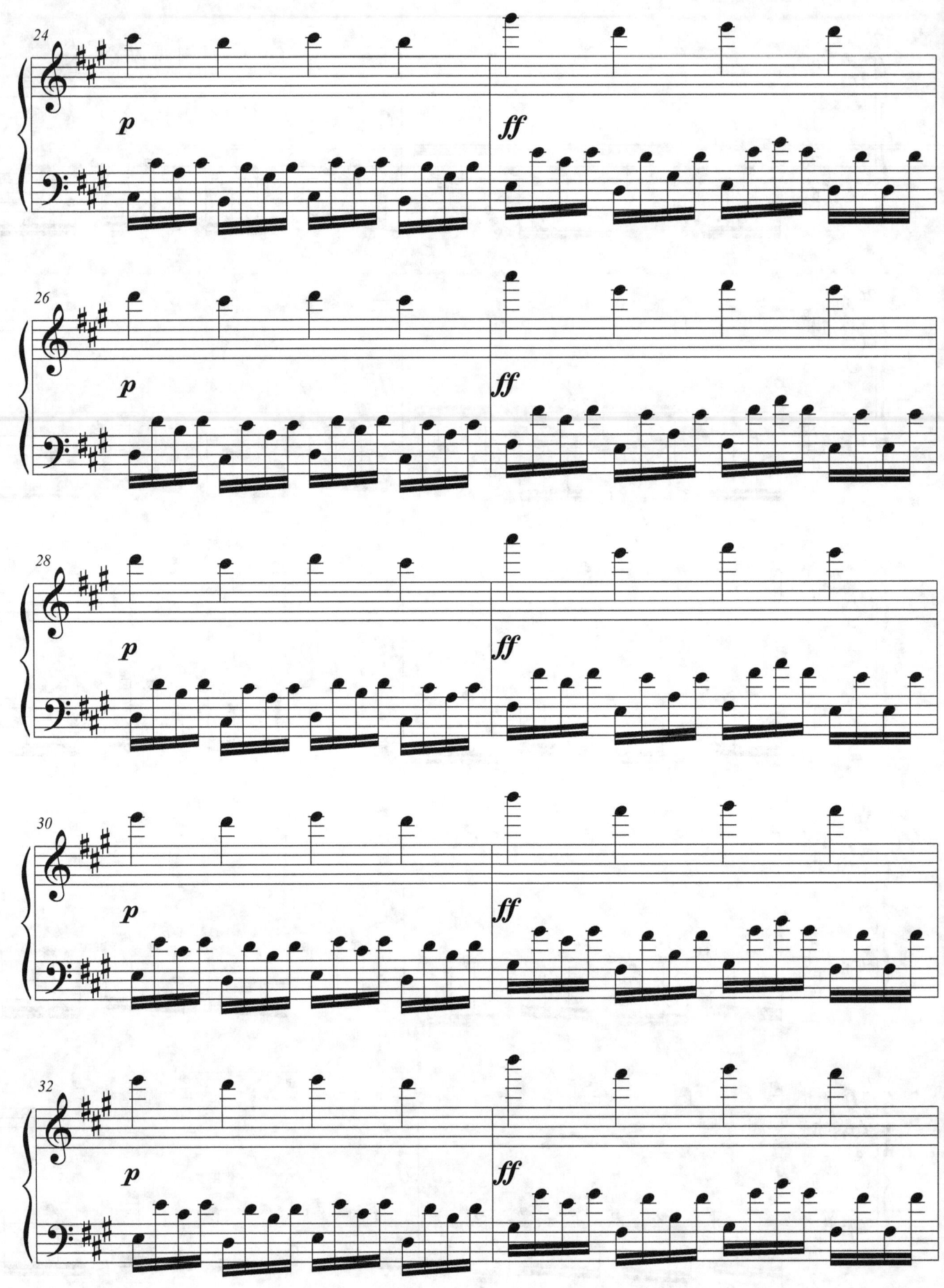

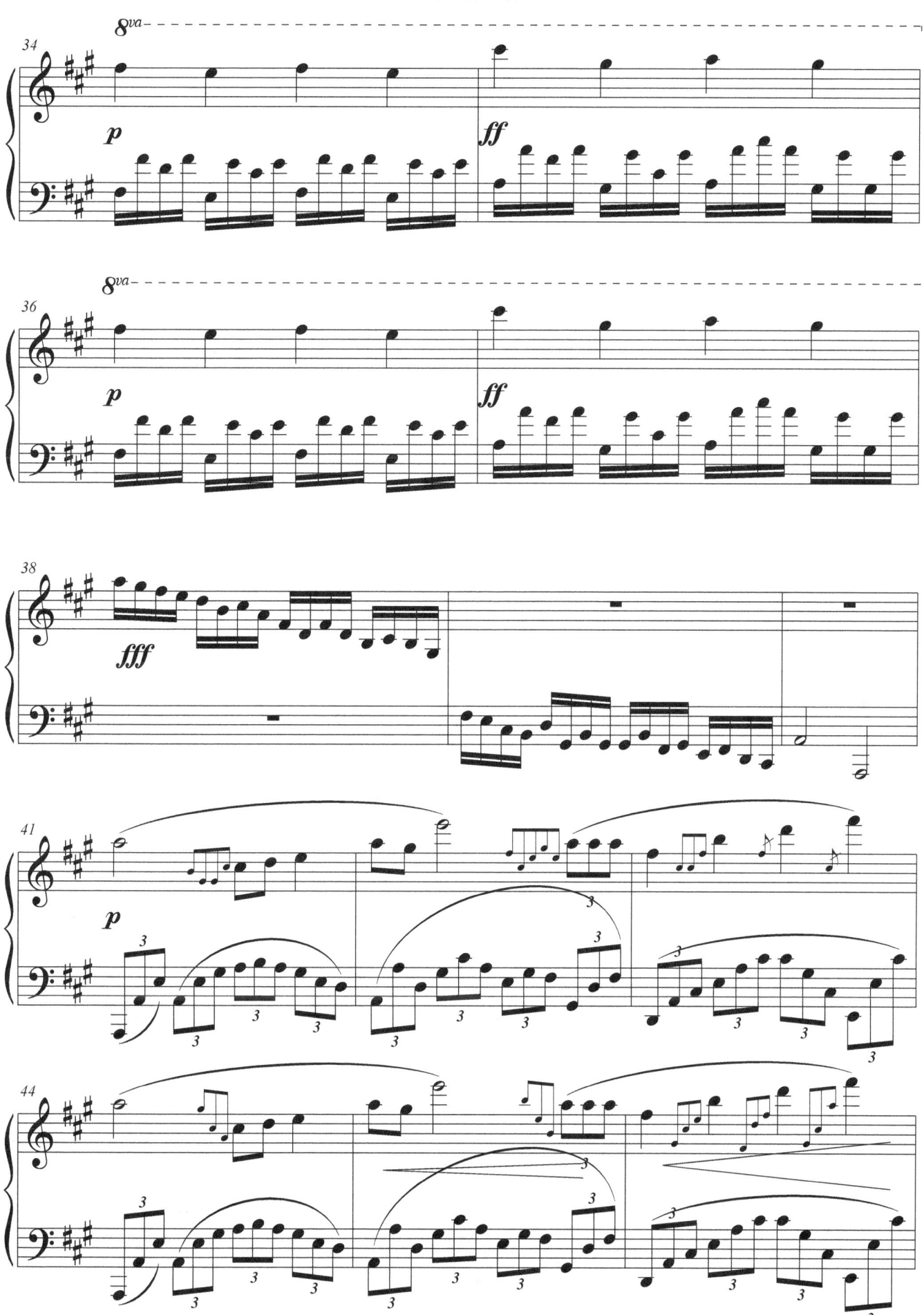

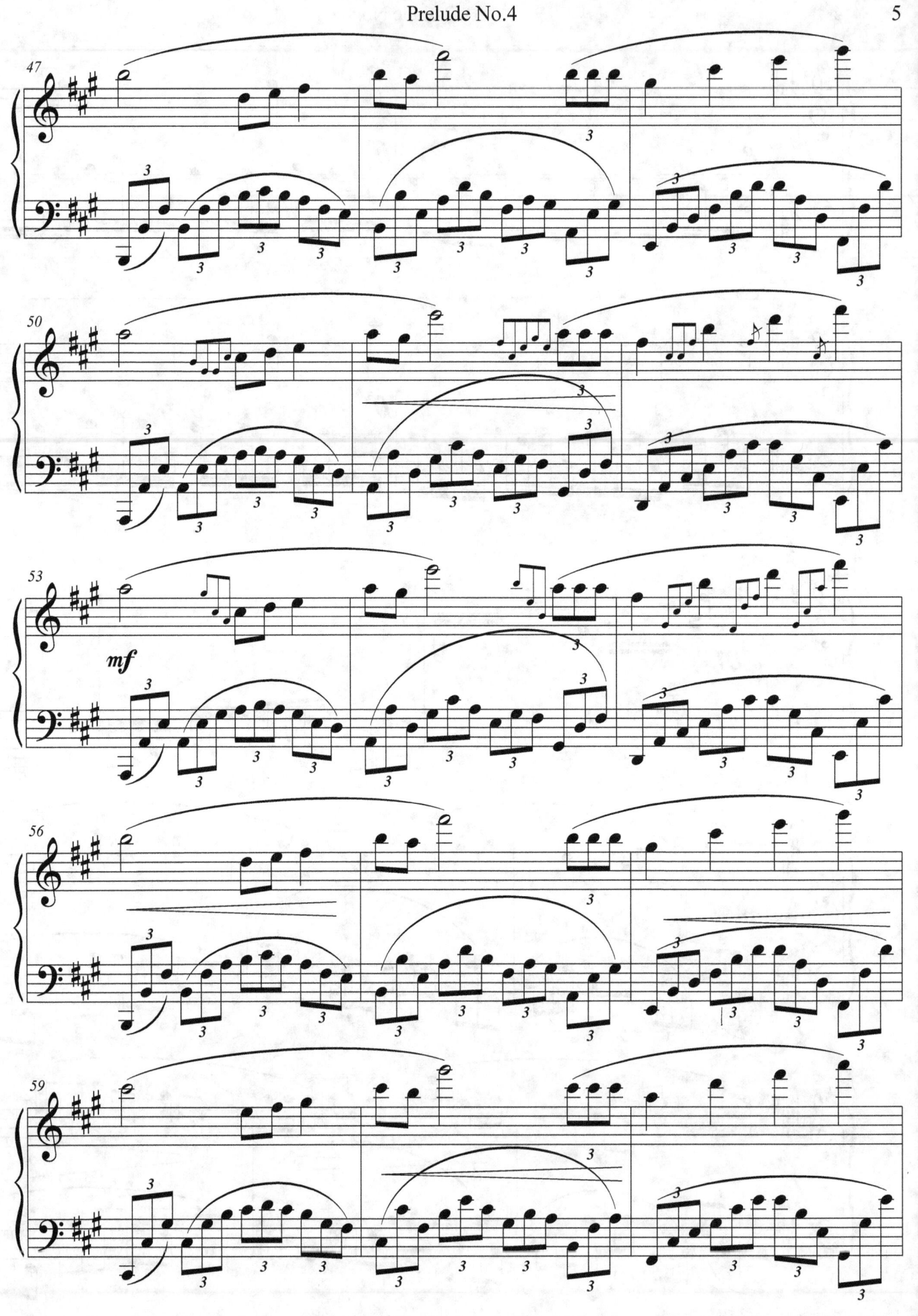

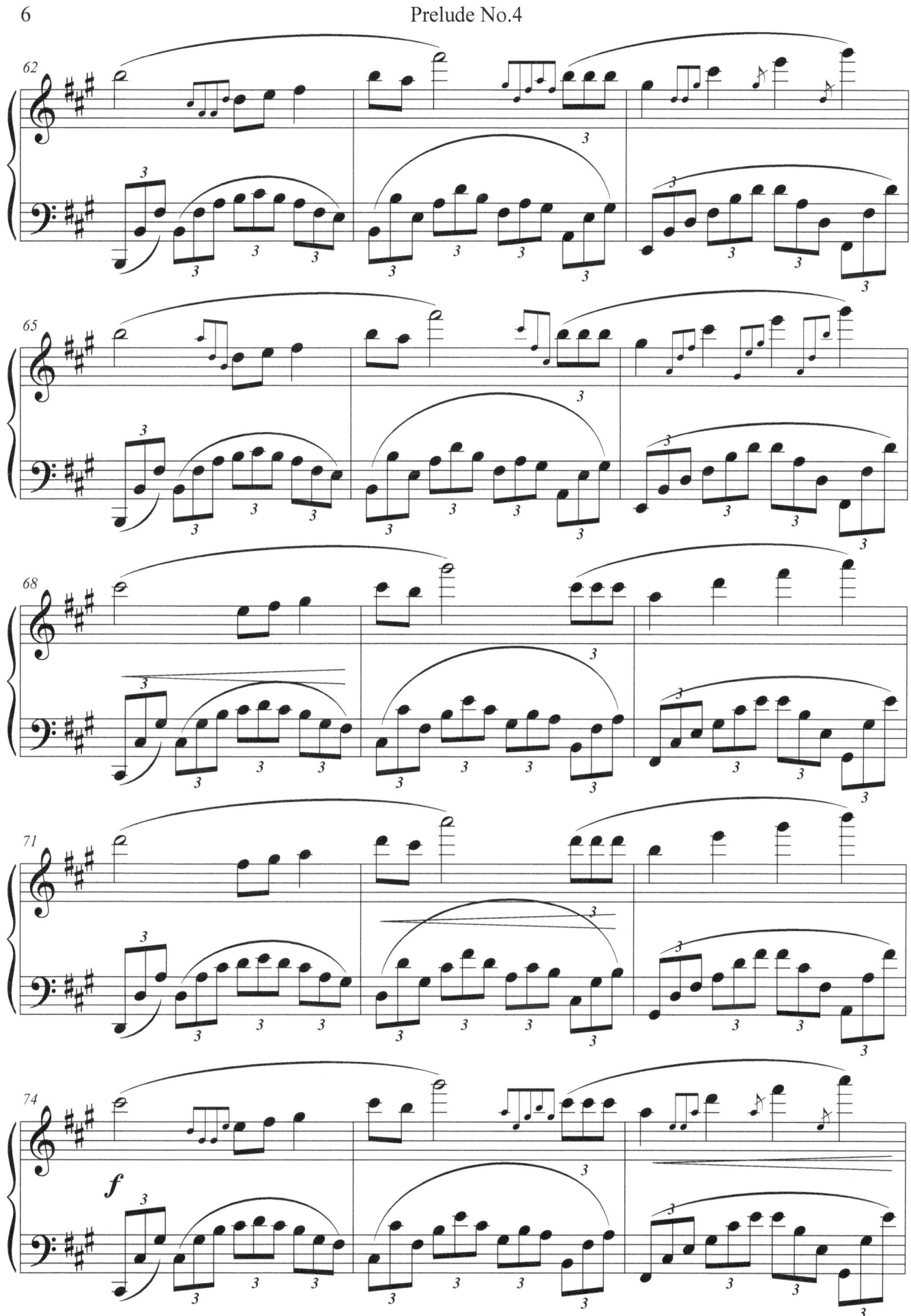

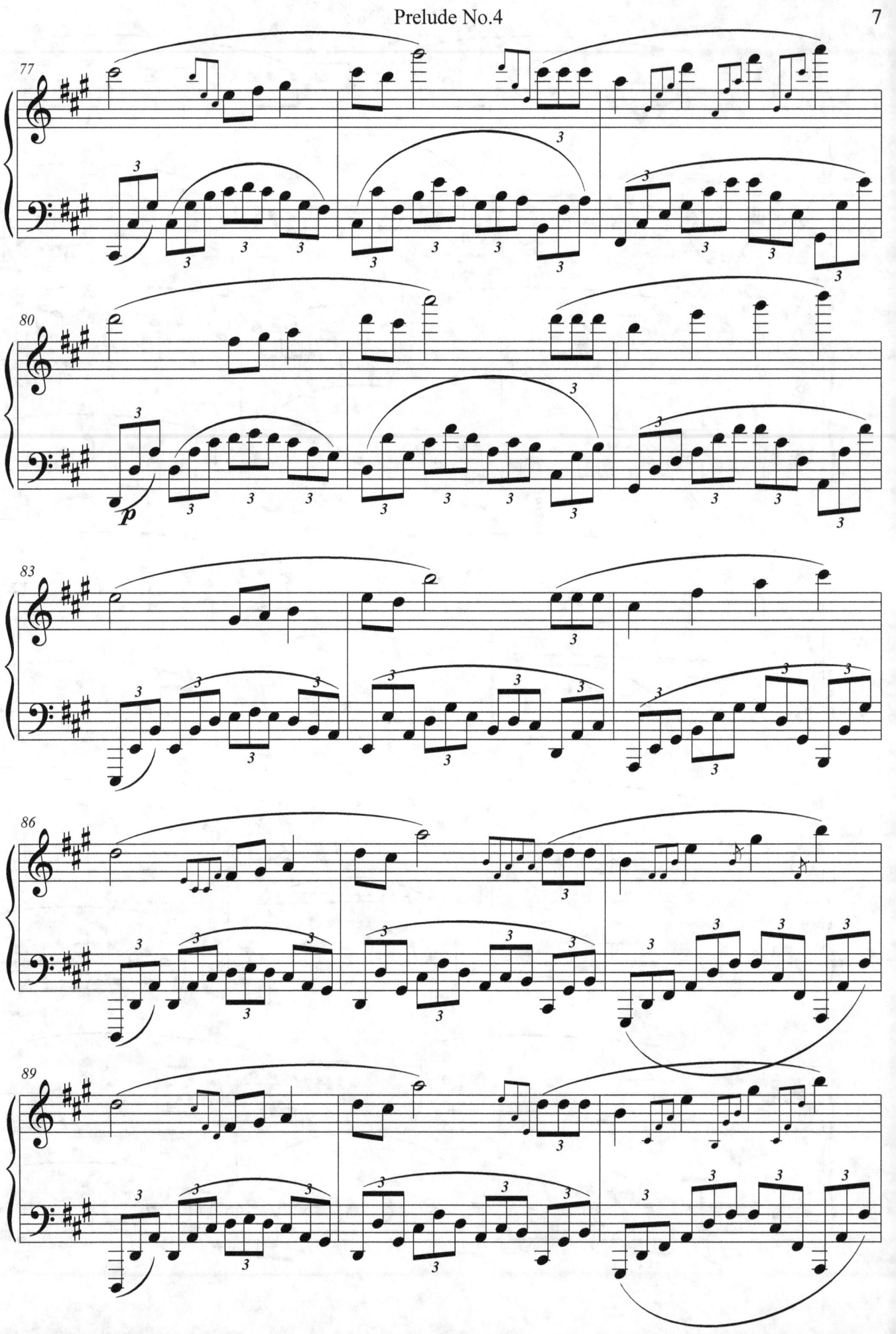

Prelude No.4

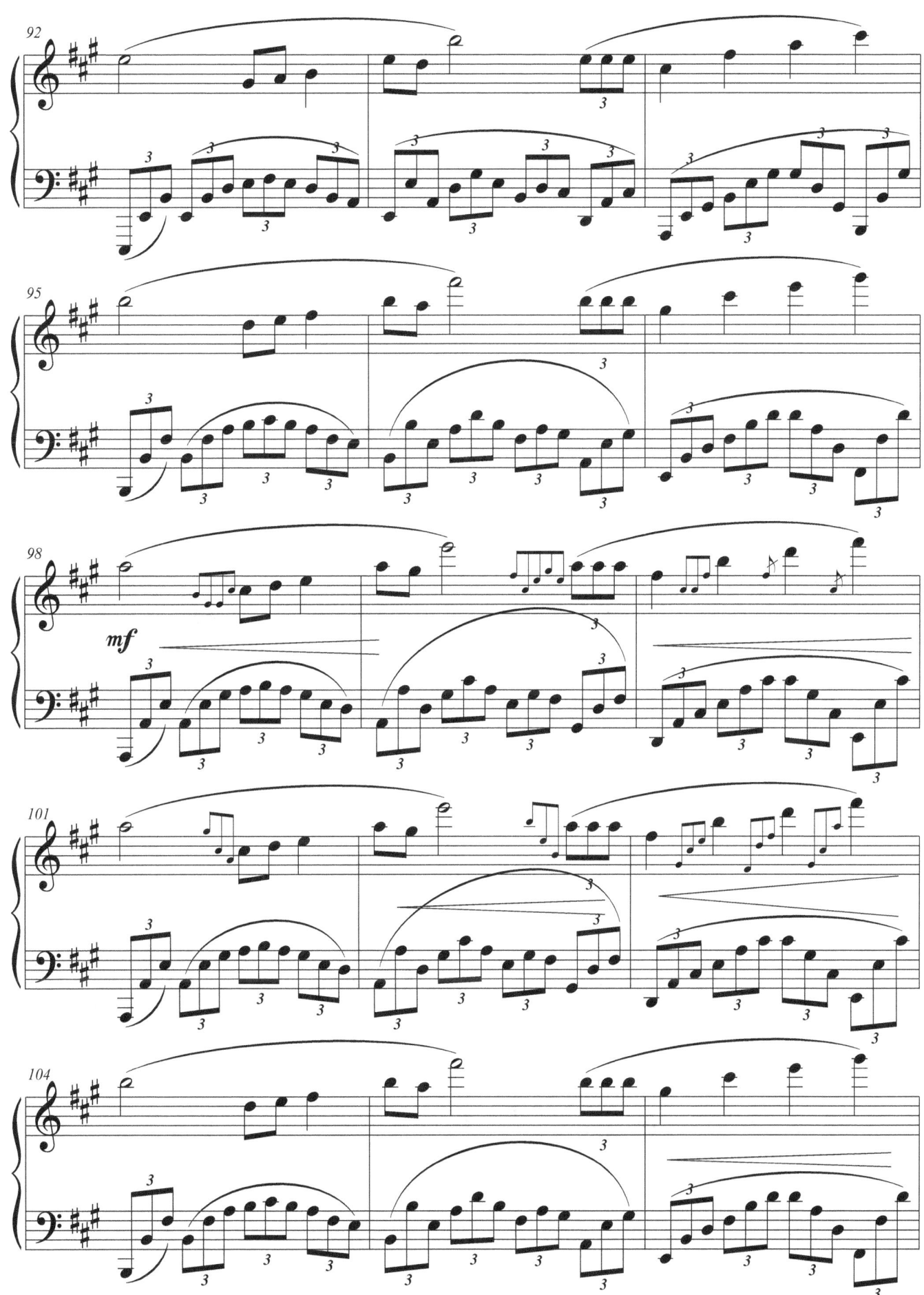

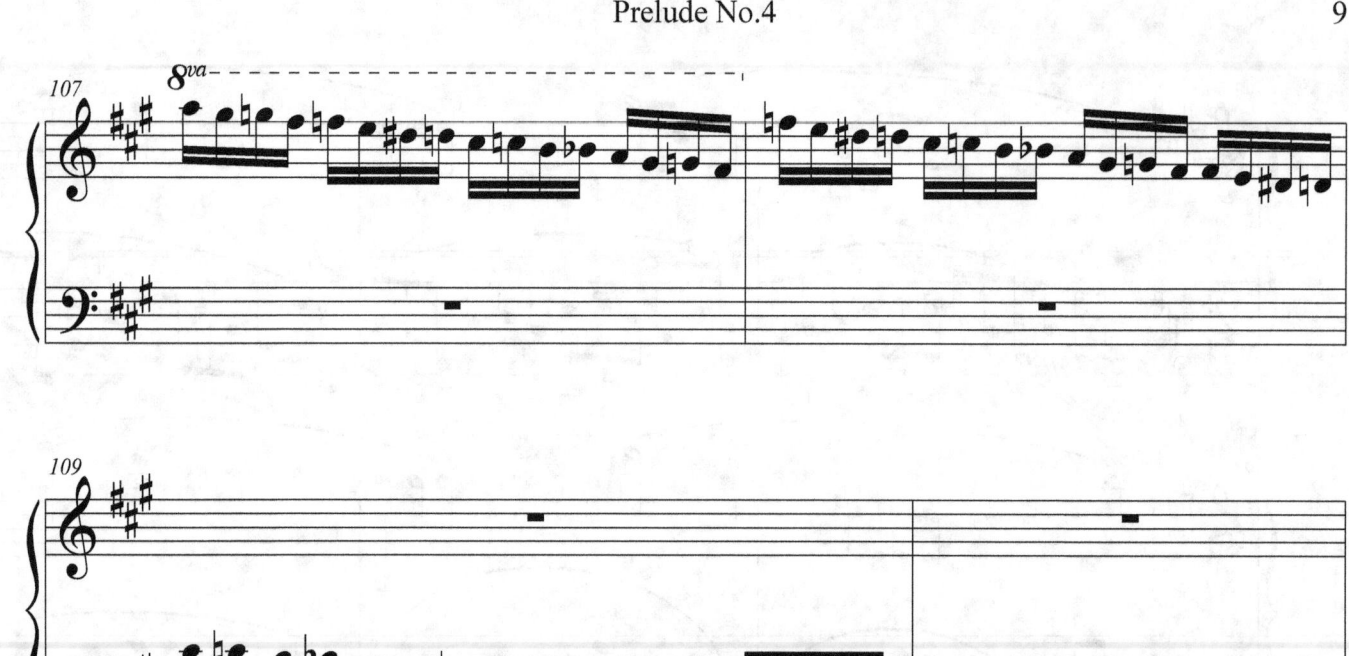

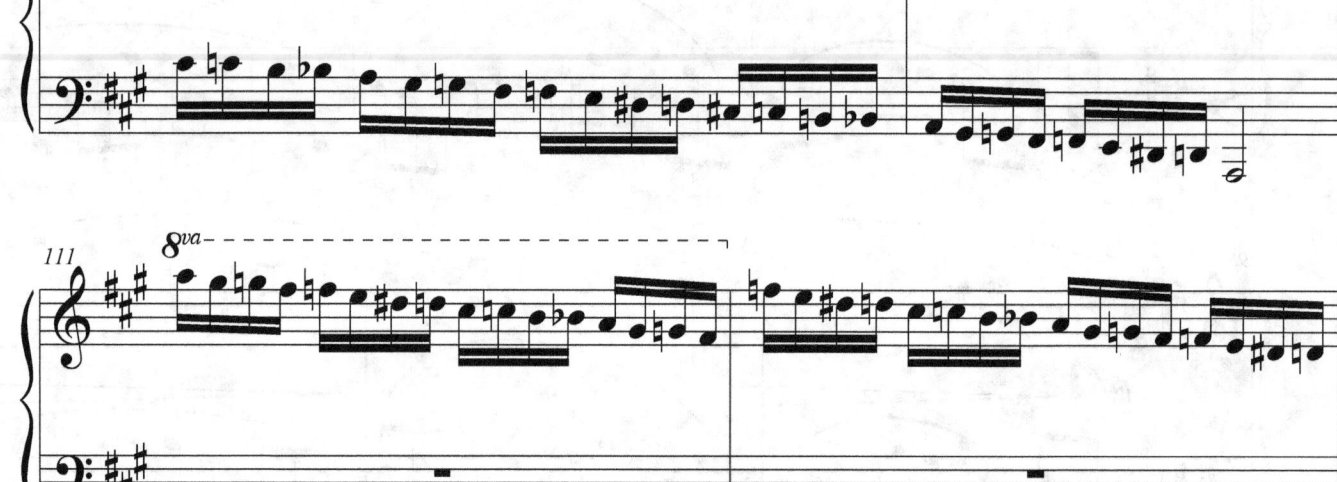

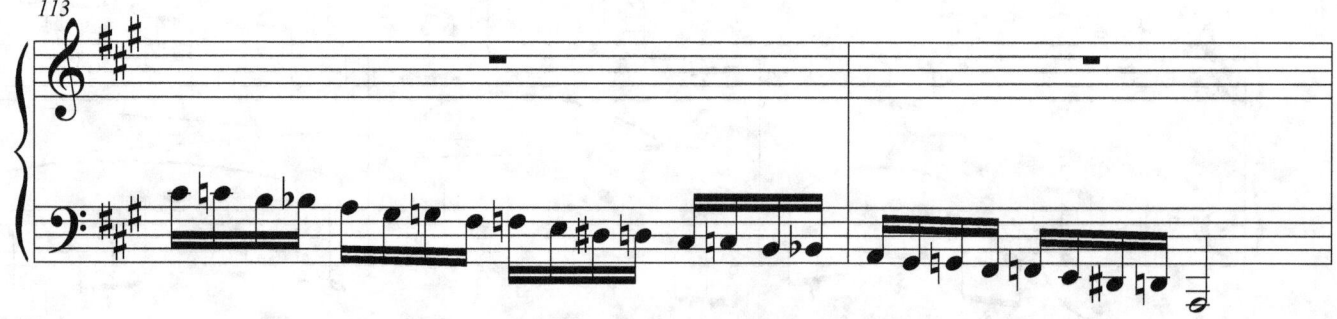

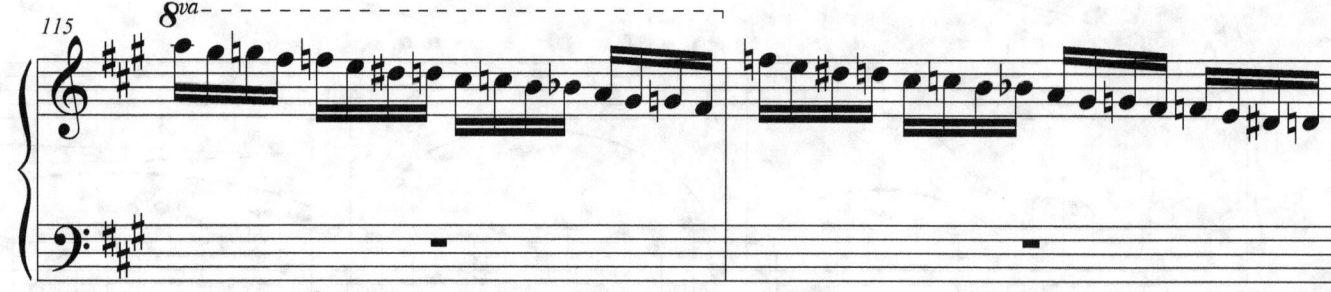

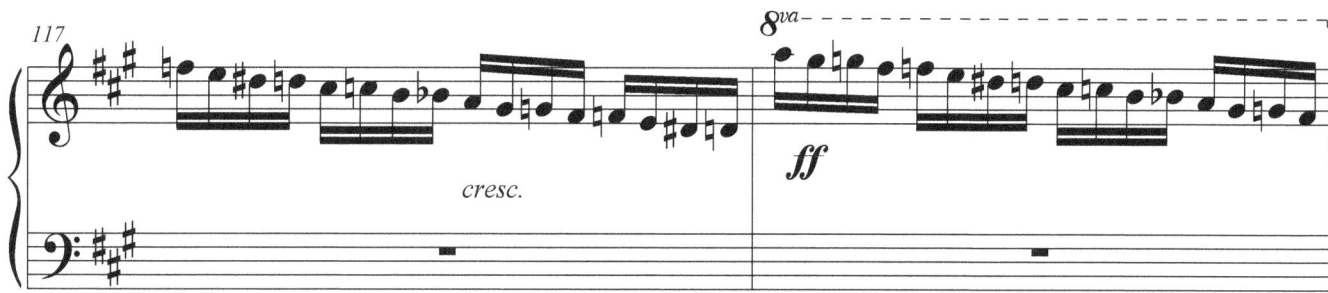

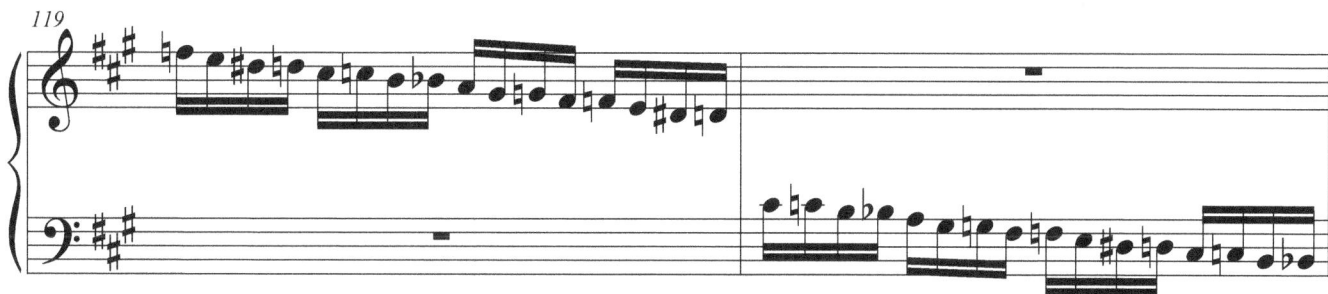

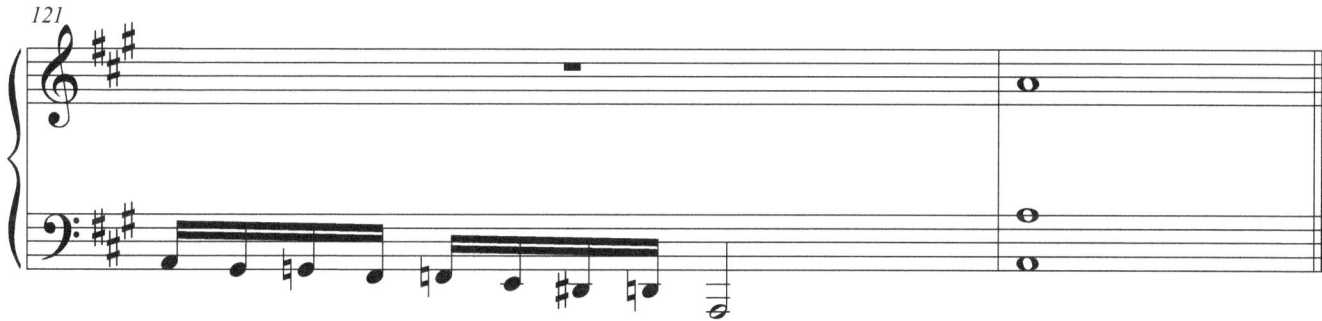

Prelude No.5

Dubiell A. De Zarraga Lago

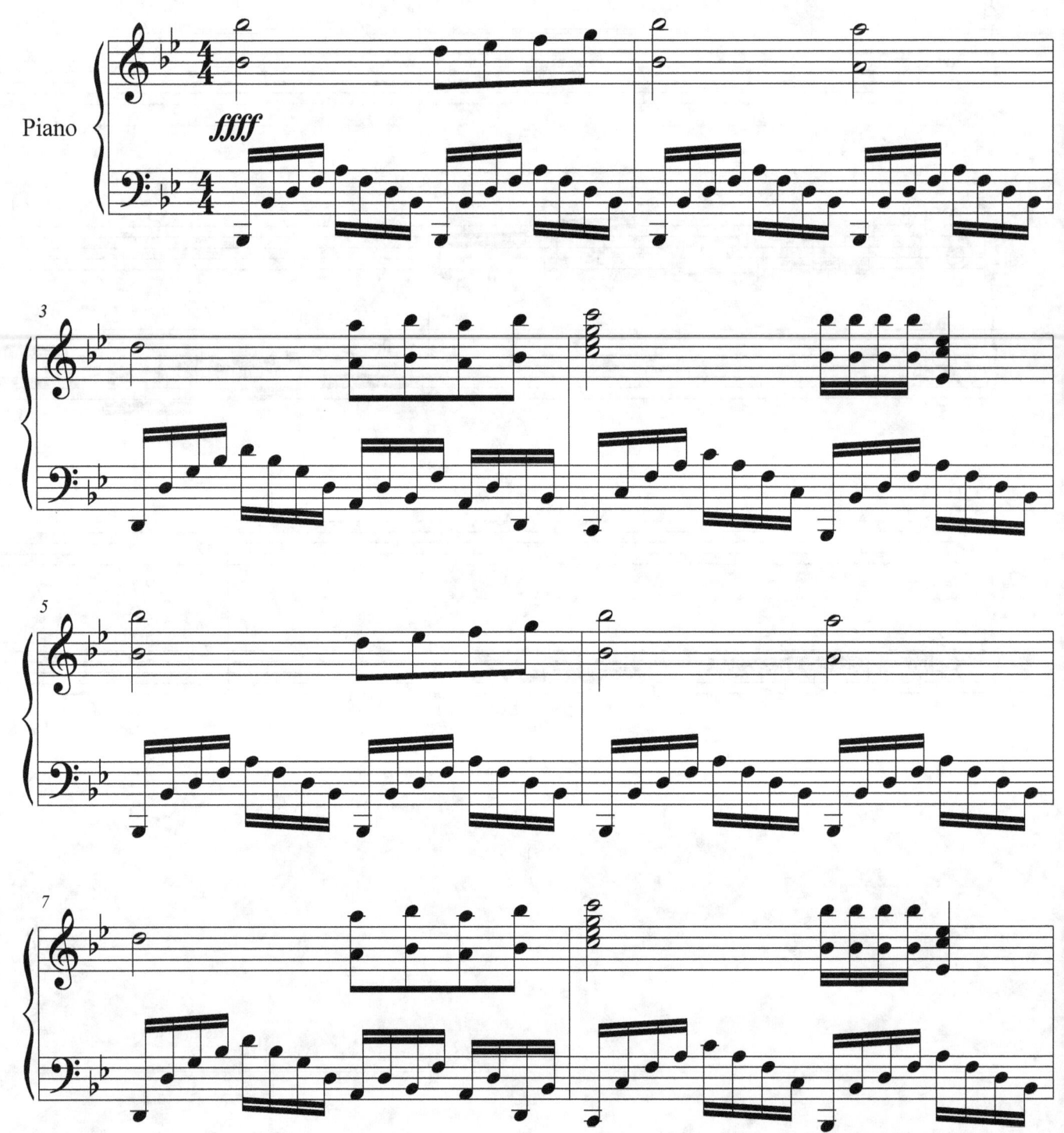

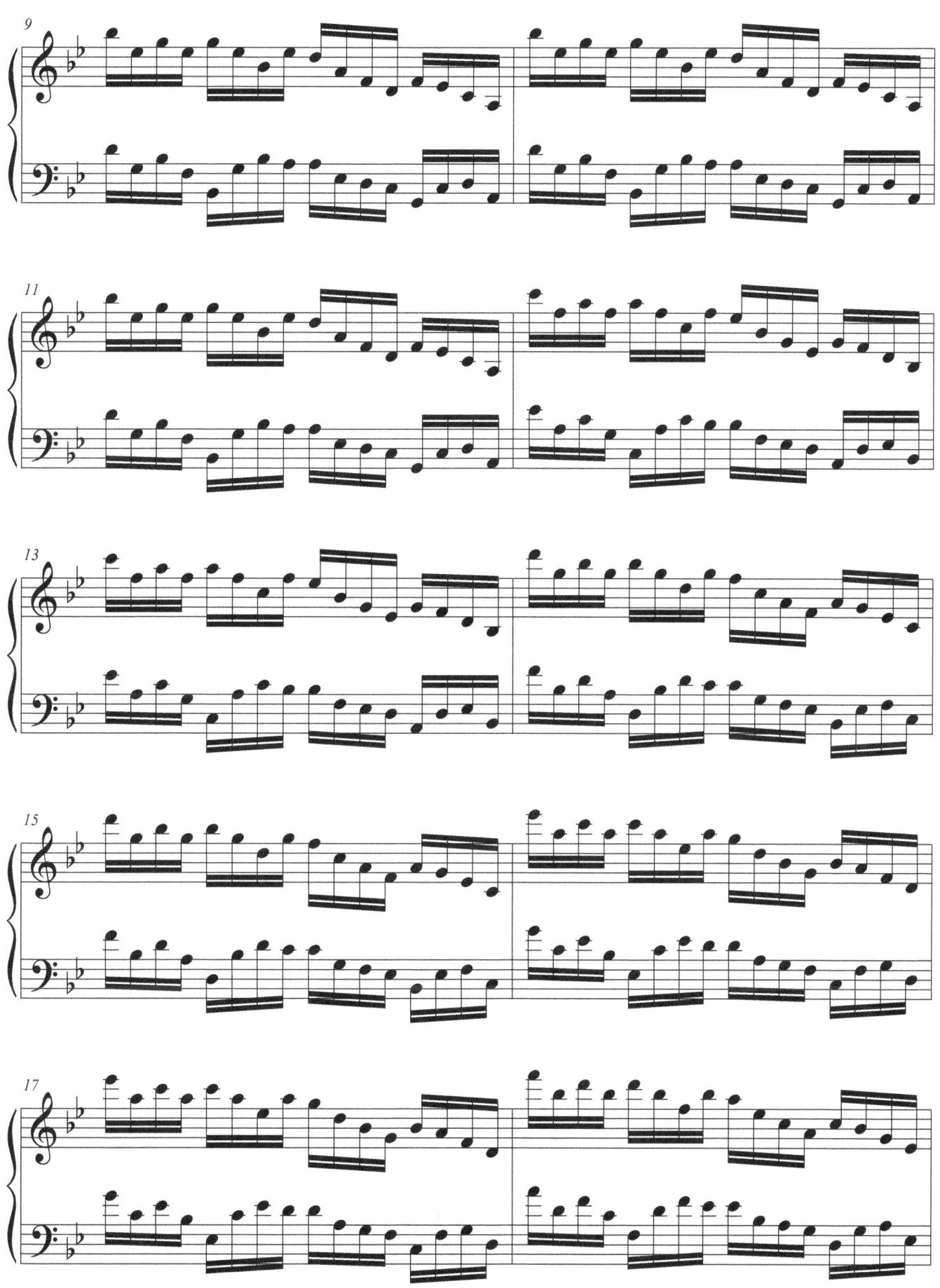

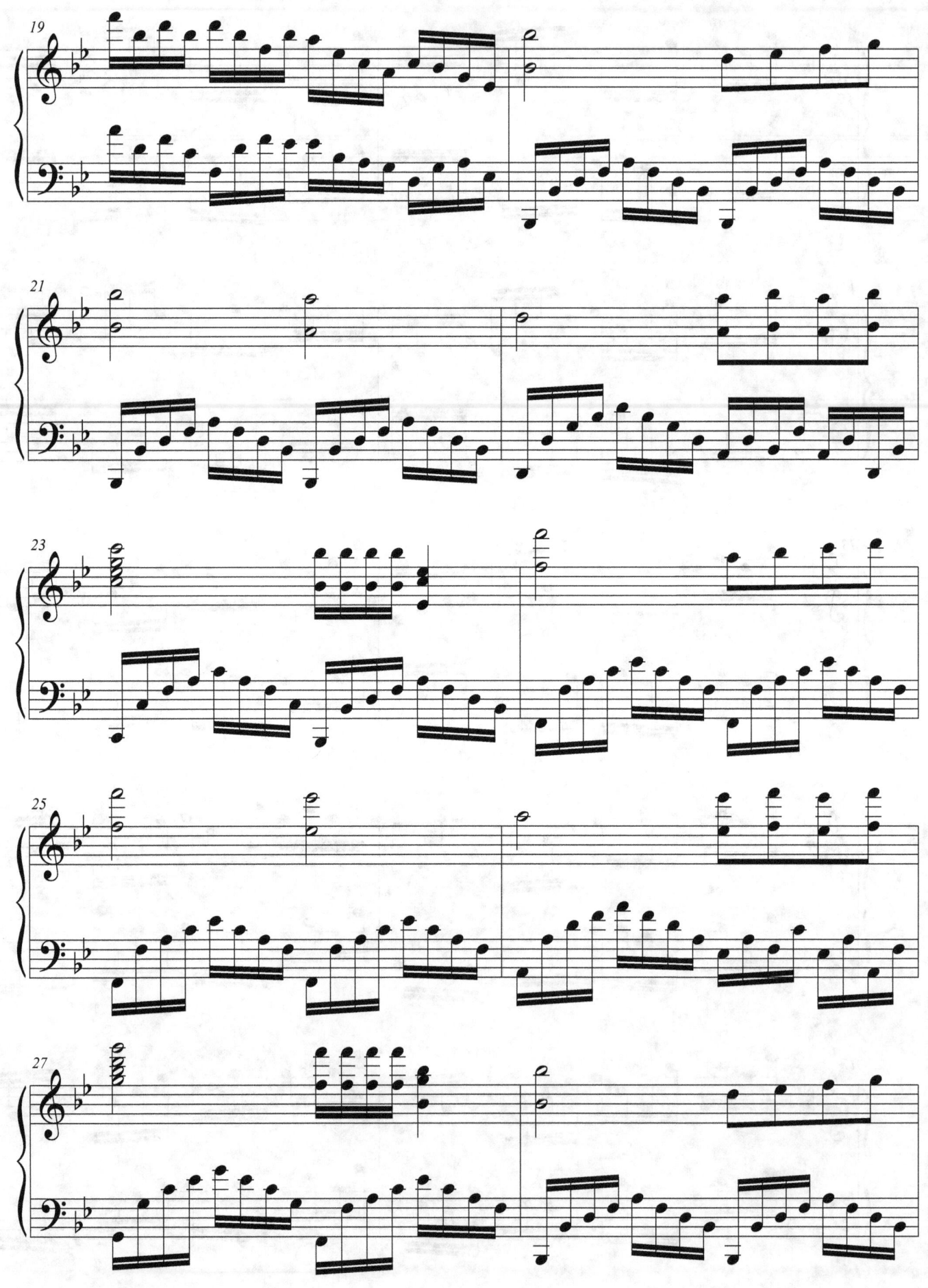

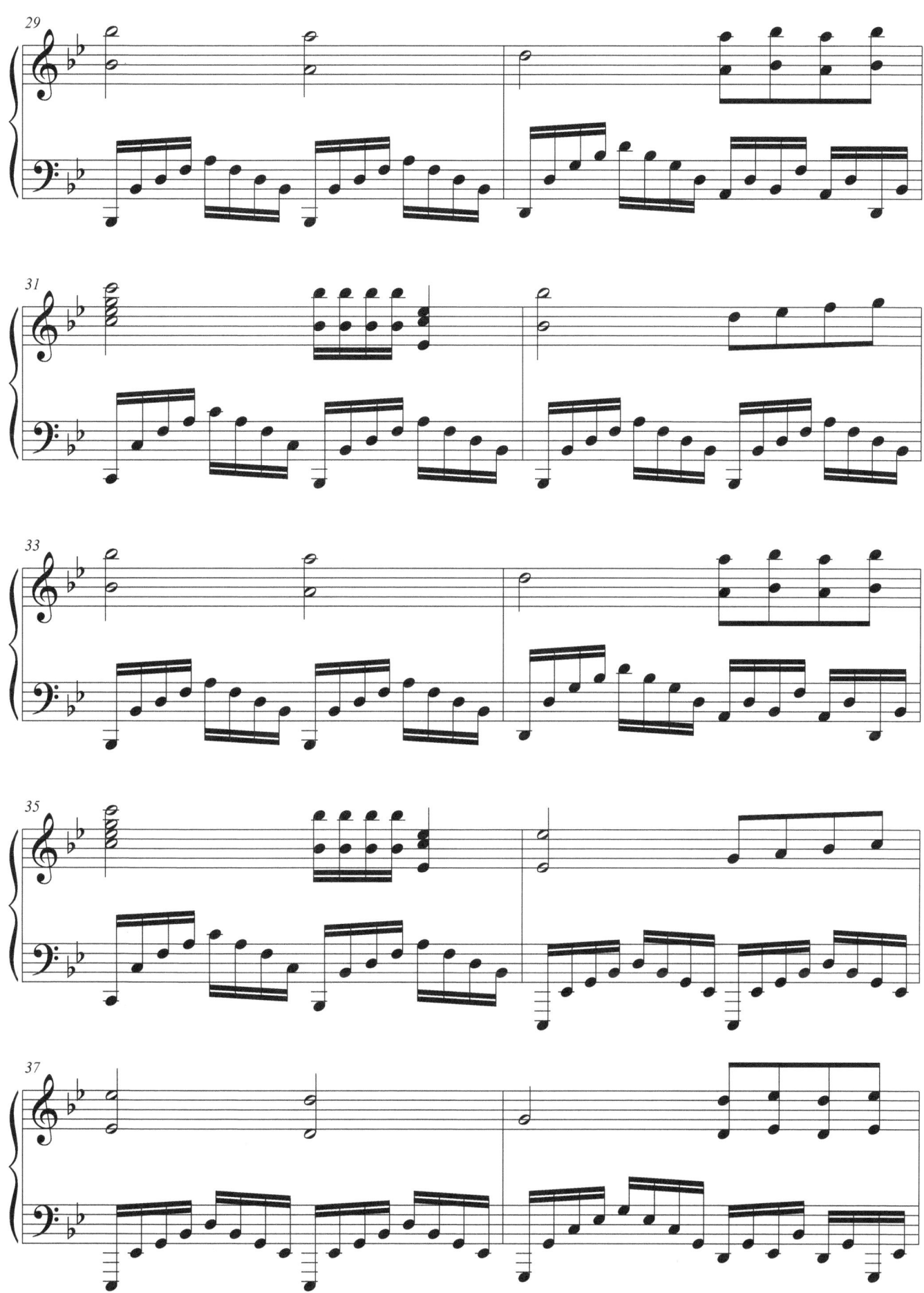

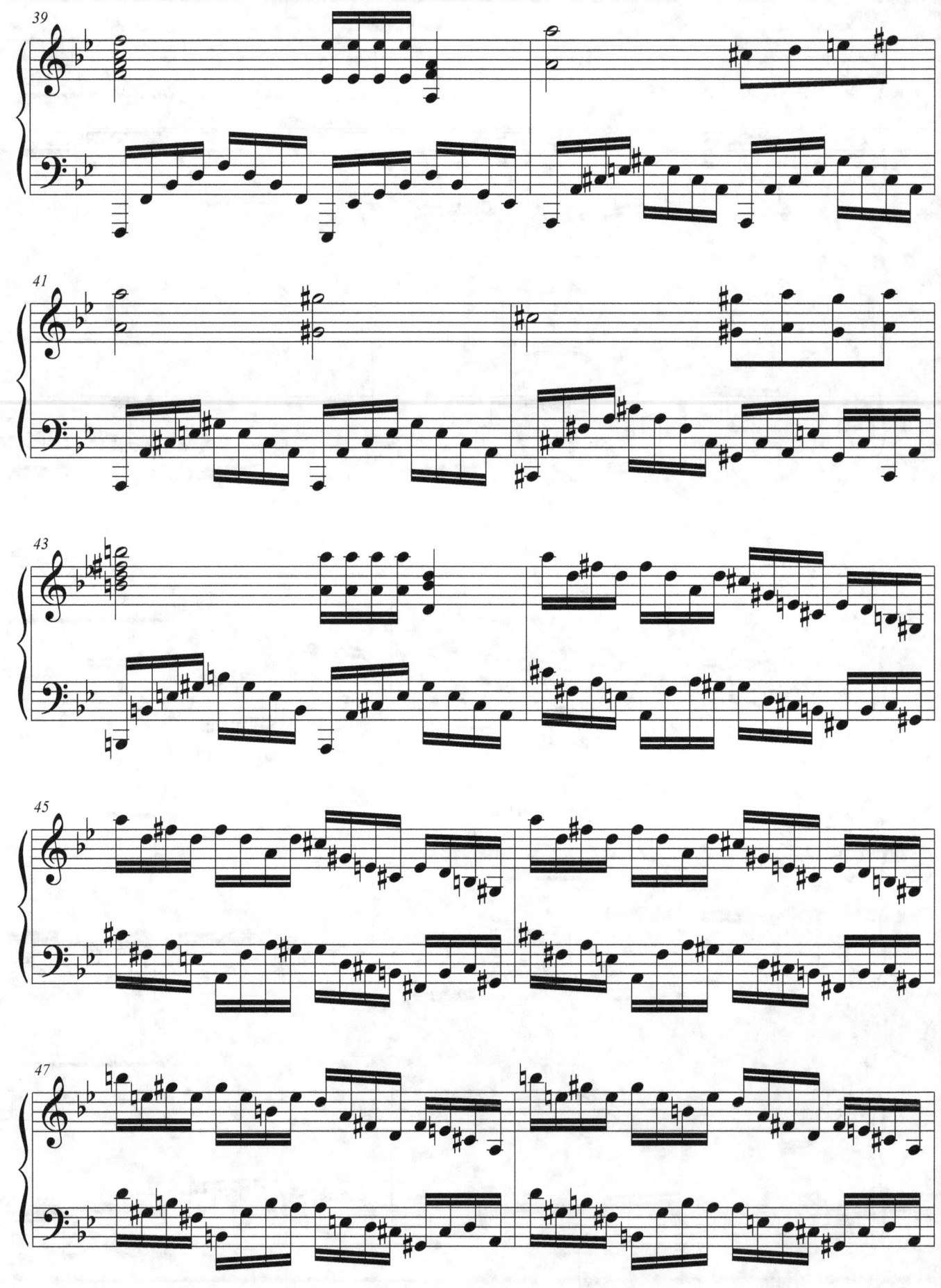

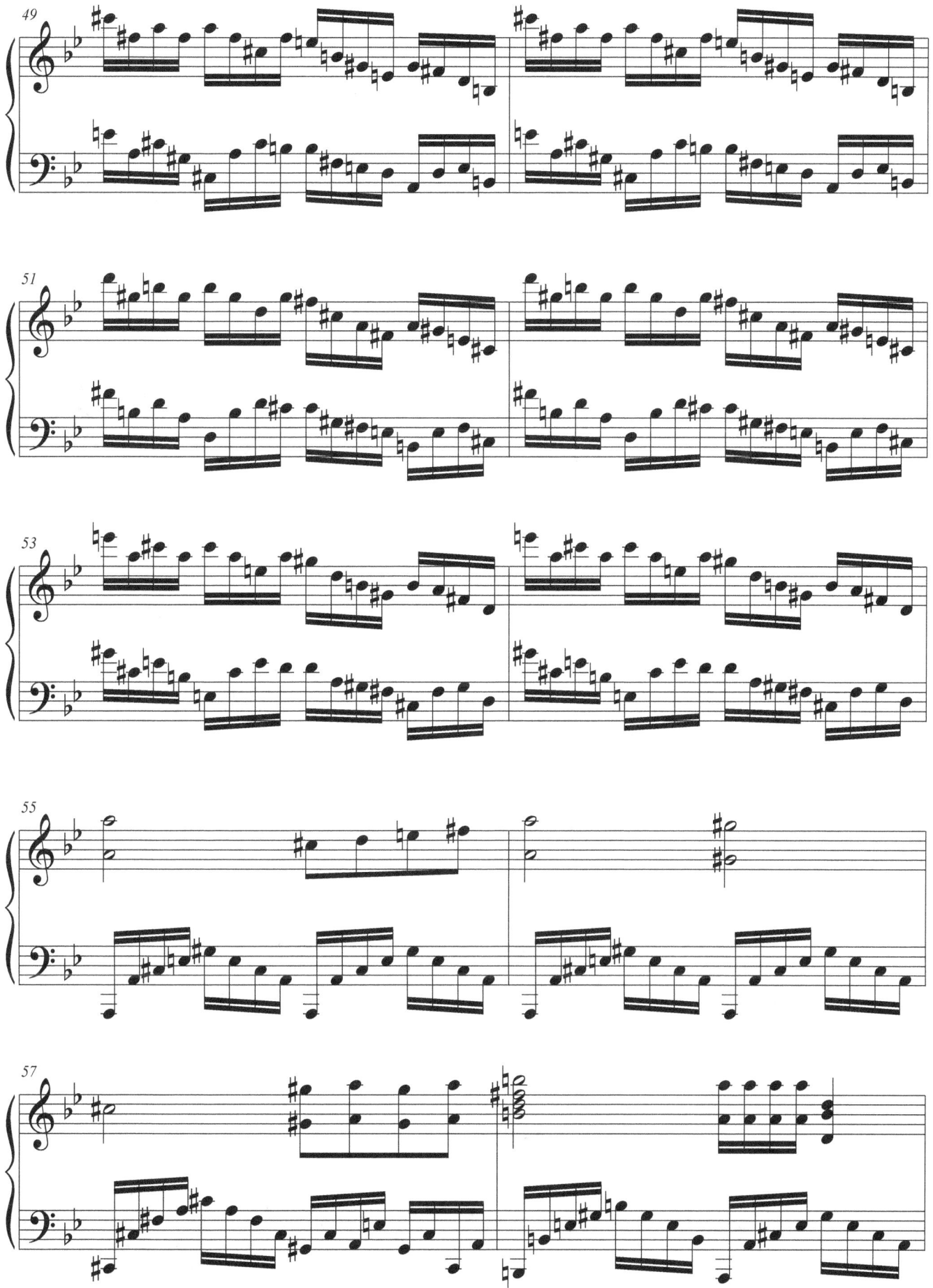

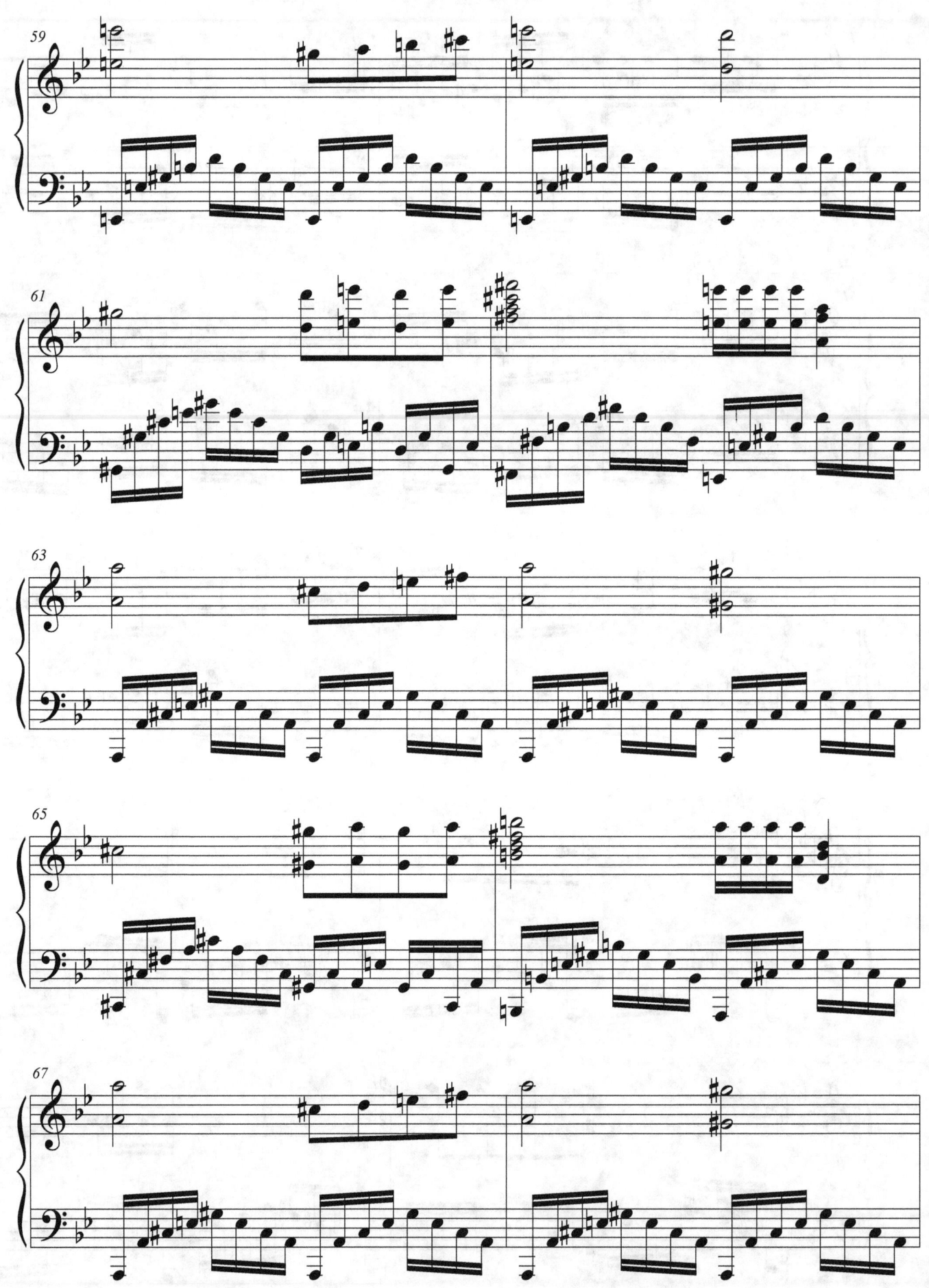

Prelude No.5

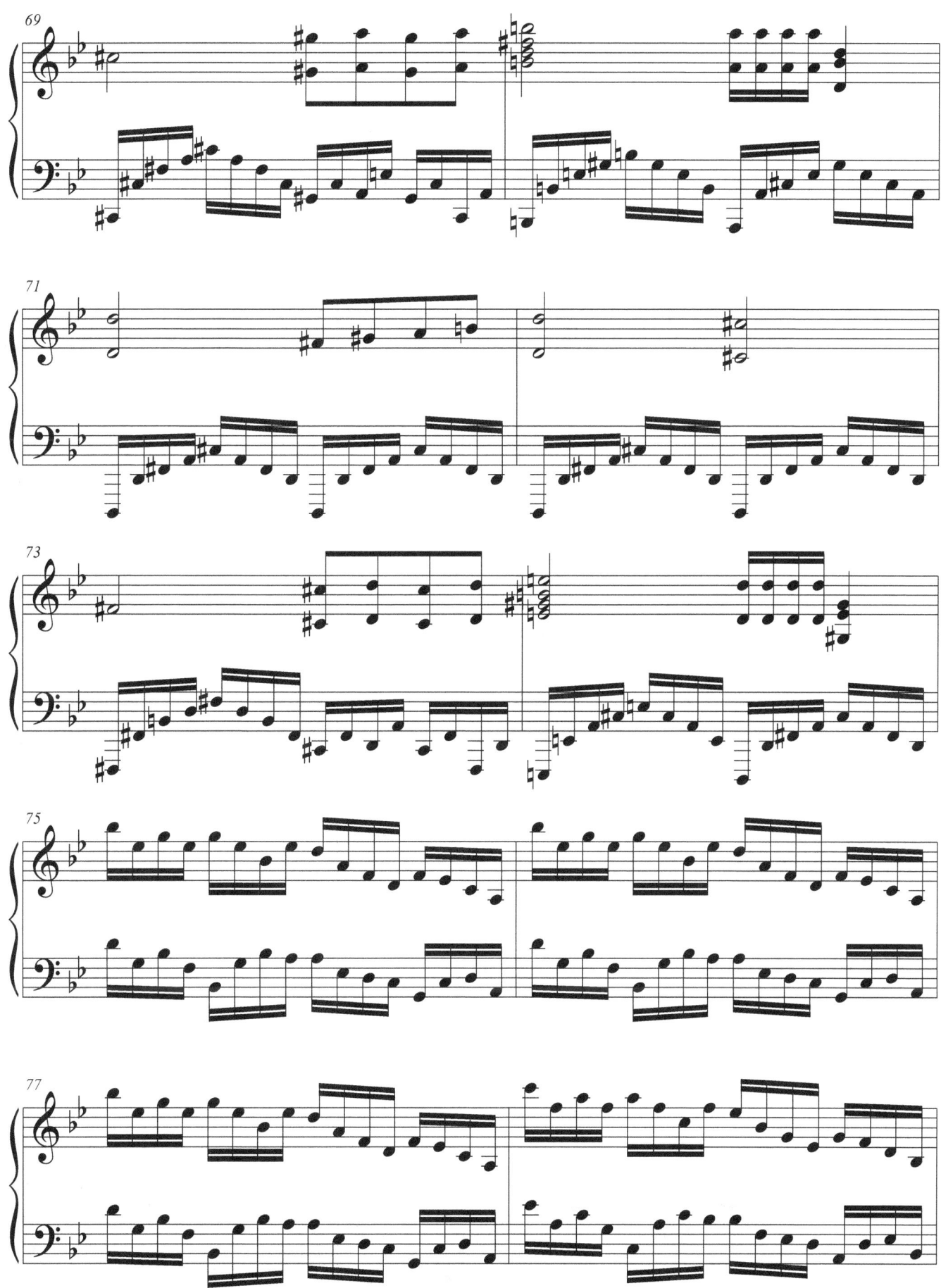

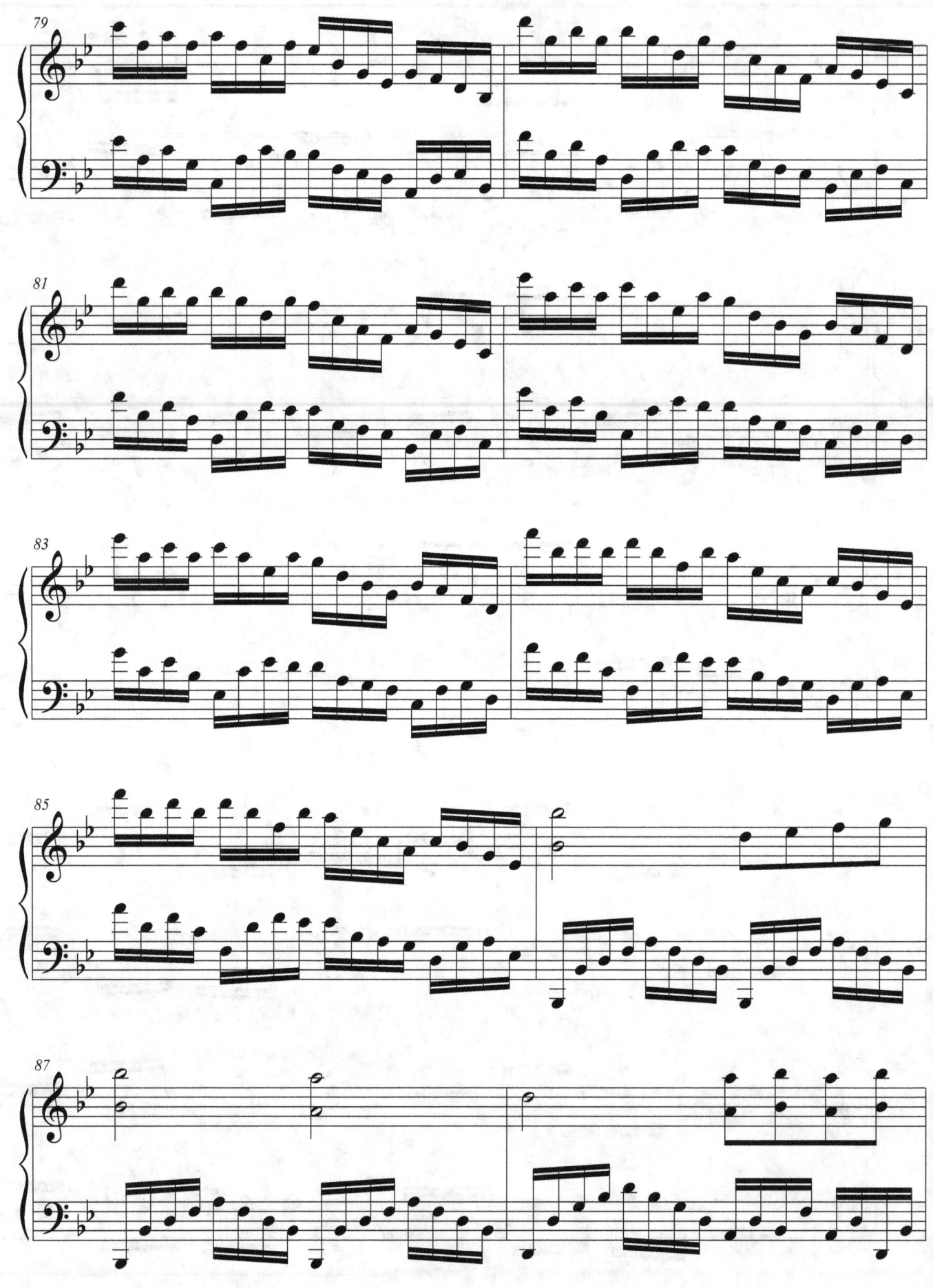

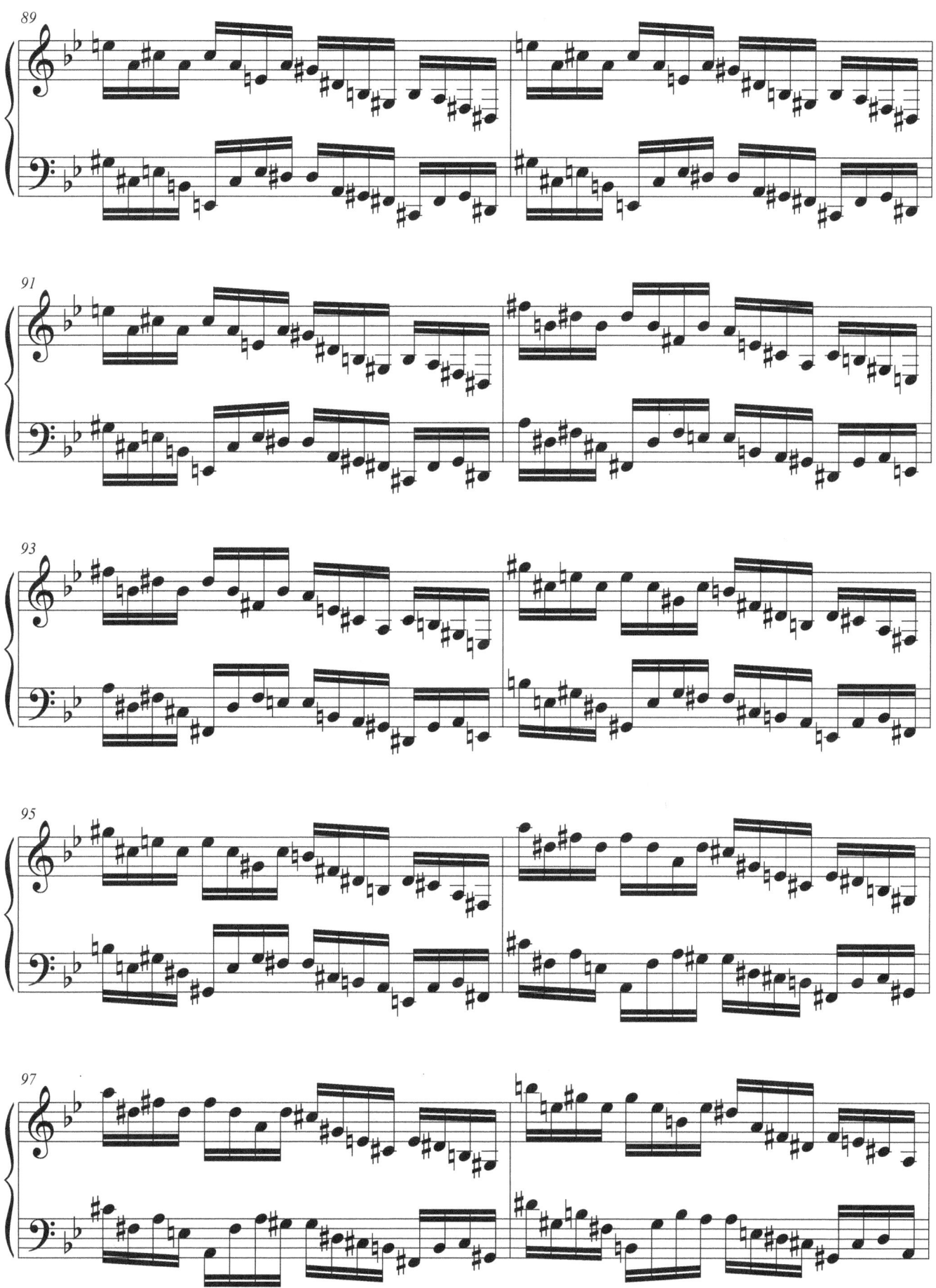

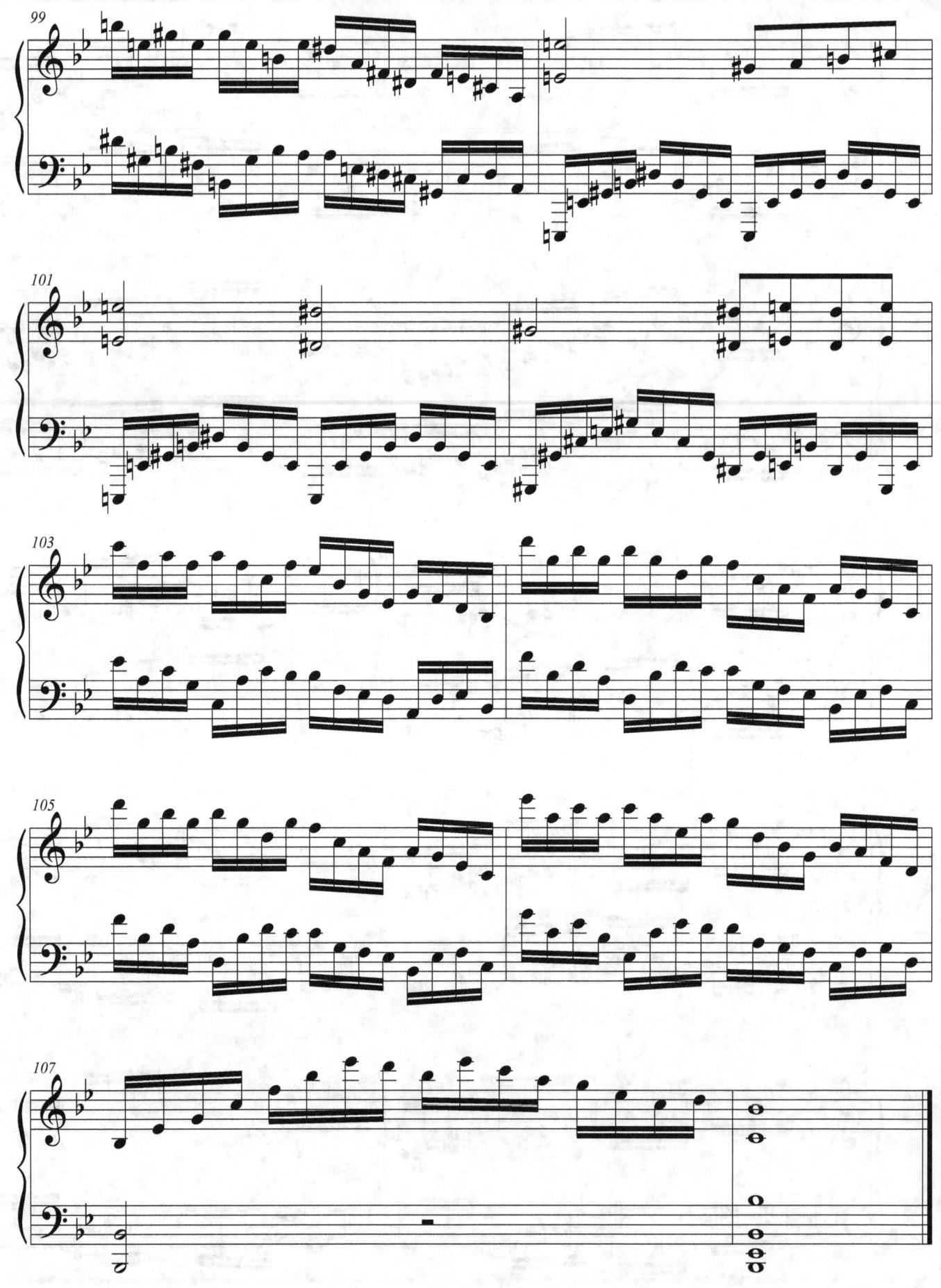

Prelude No.6

Dubiell A. De Zarraga Lago

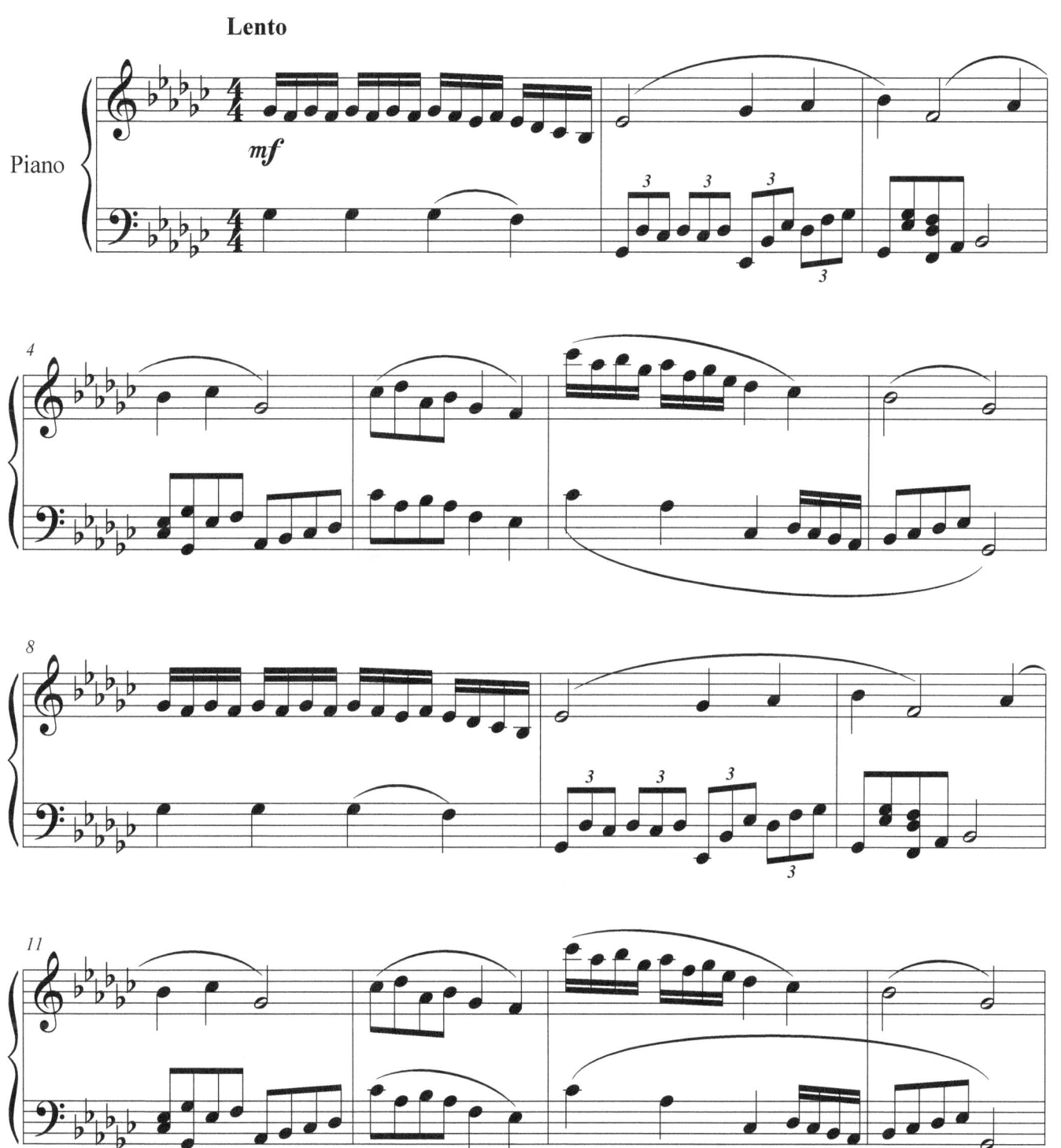

Prelude No.6

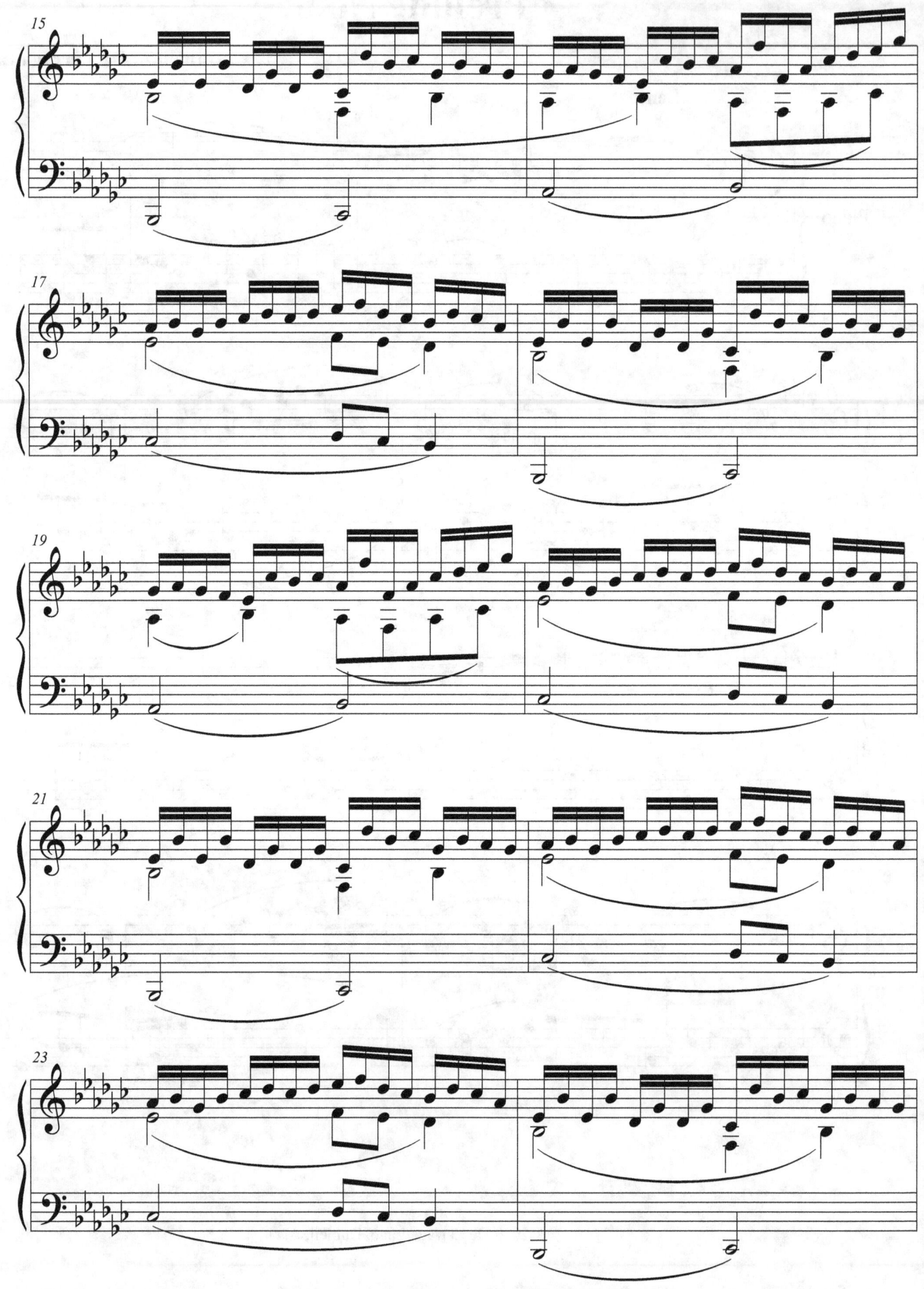

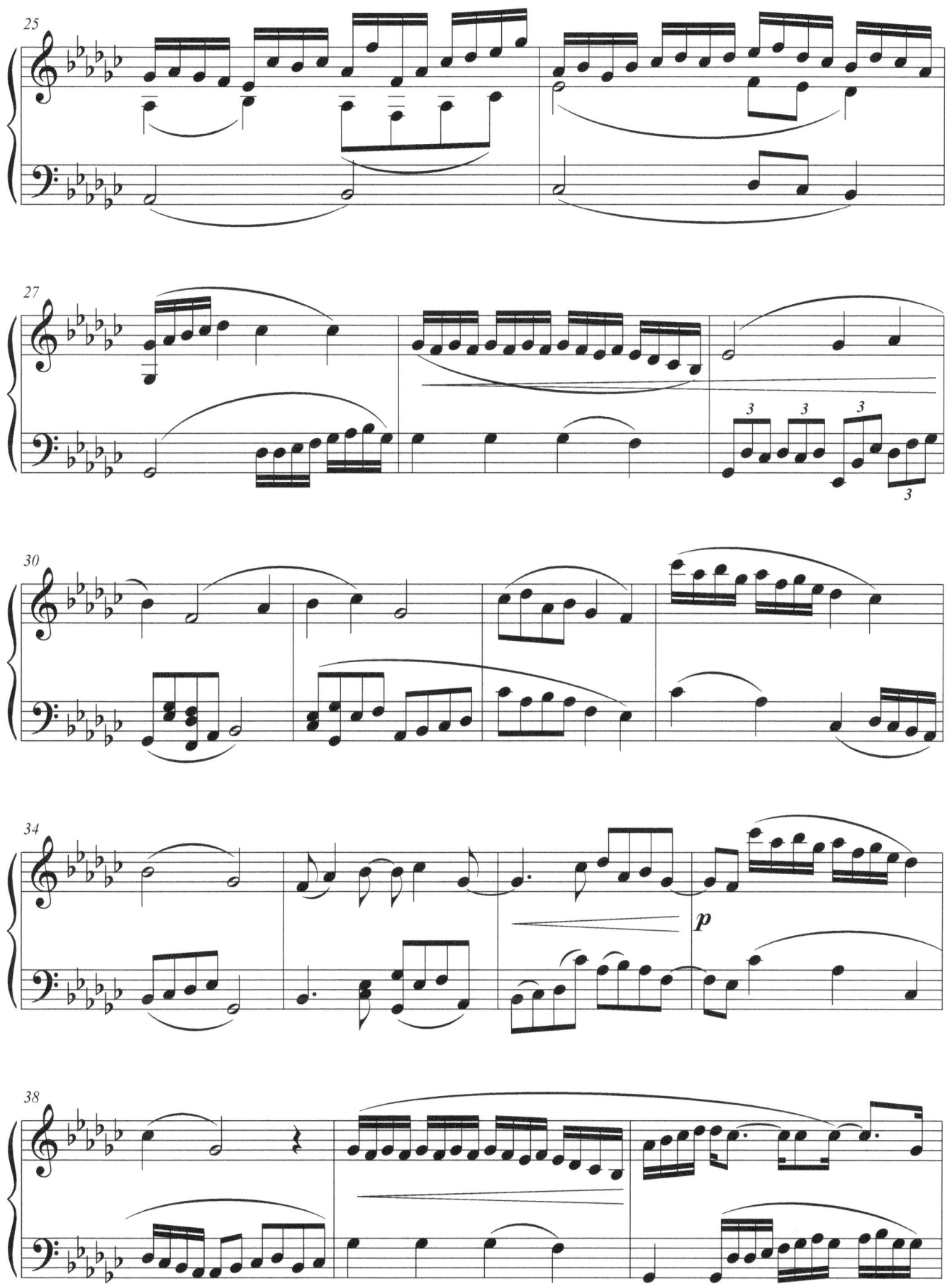

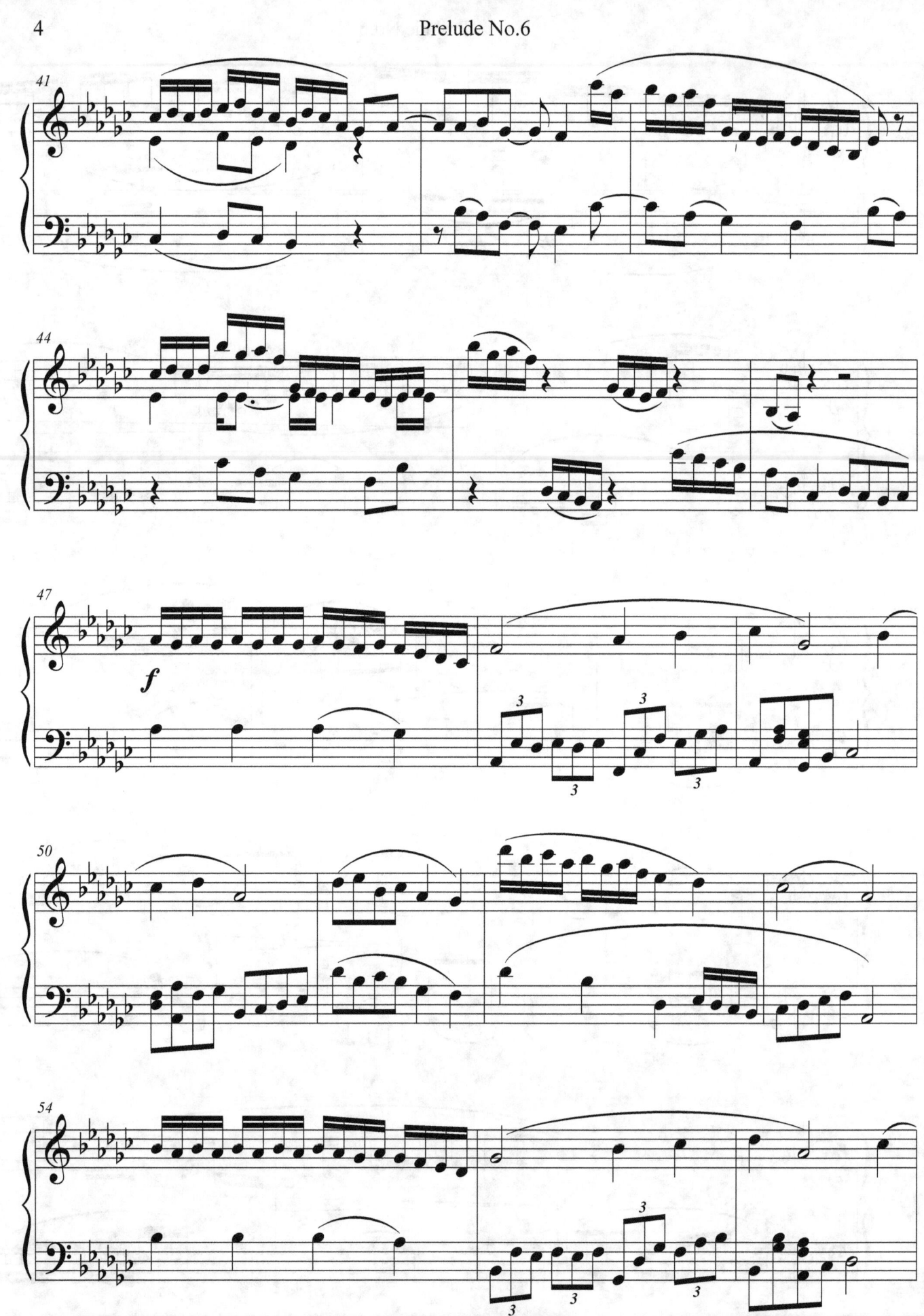

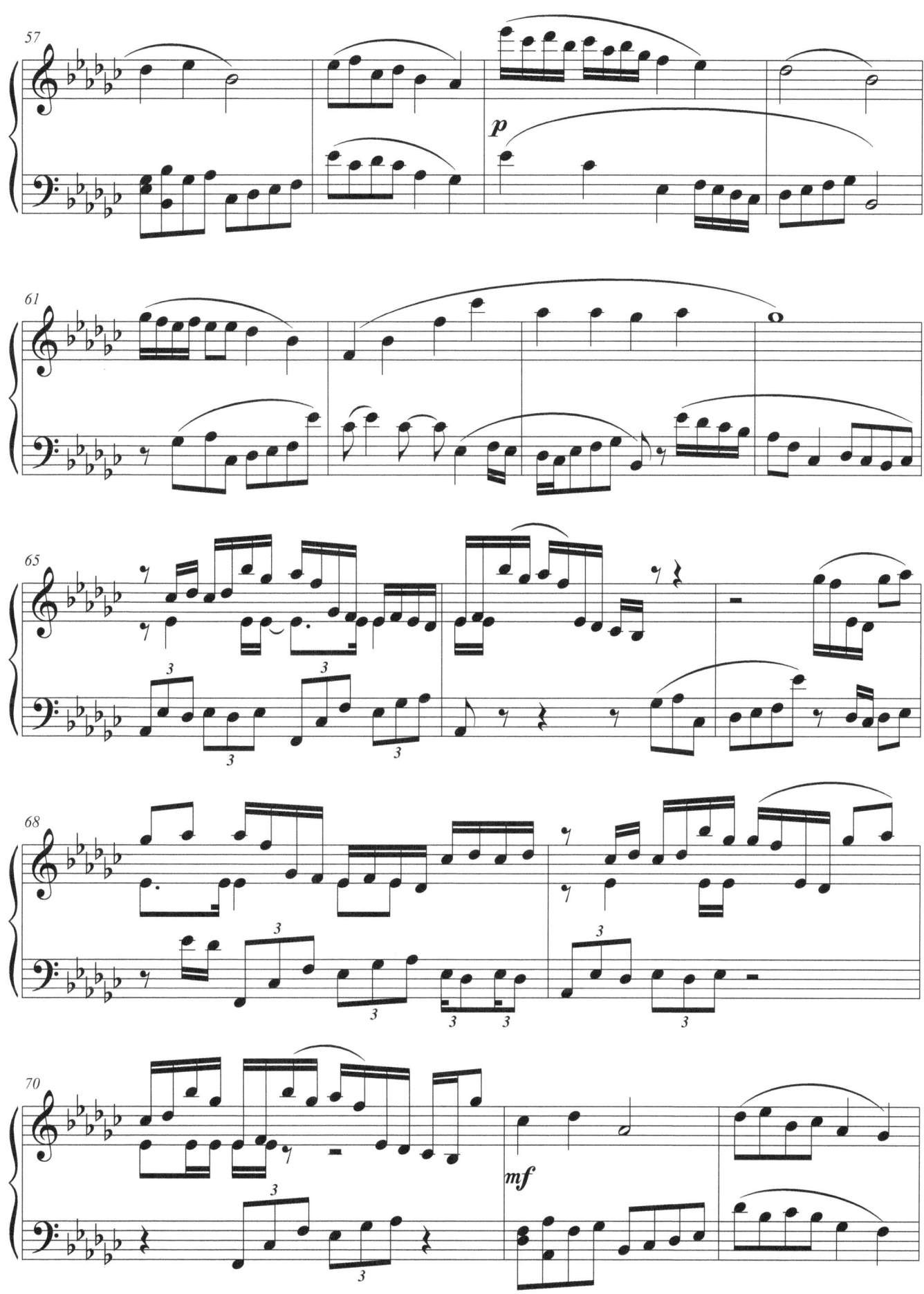

Prelude No.6

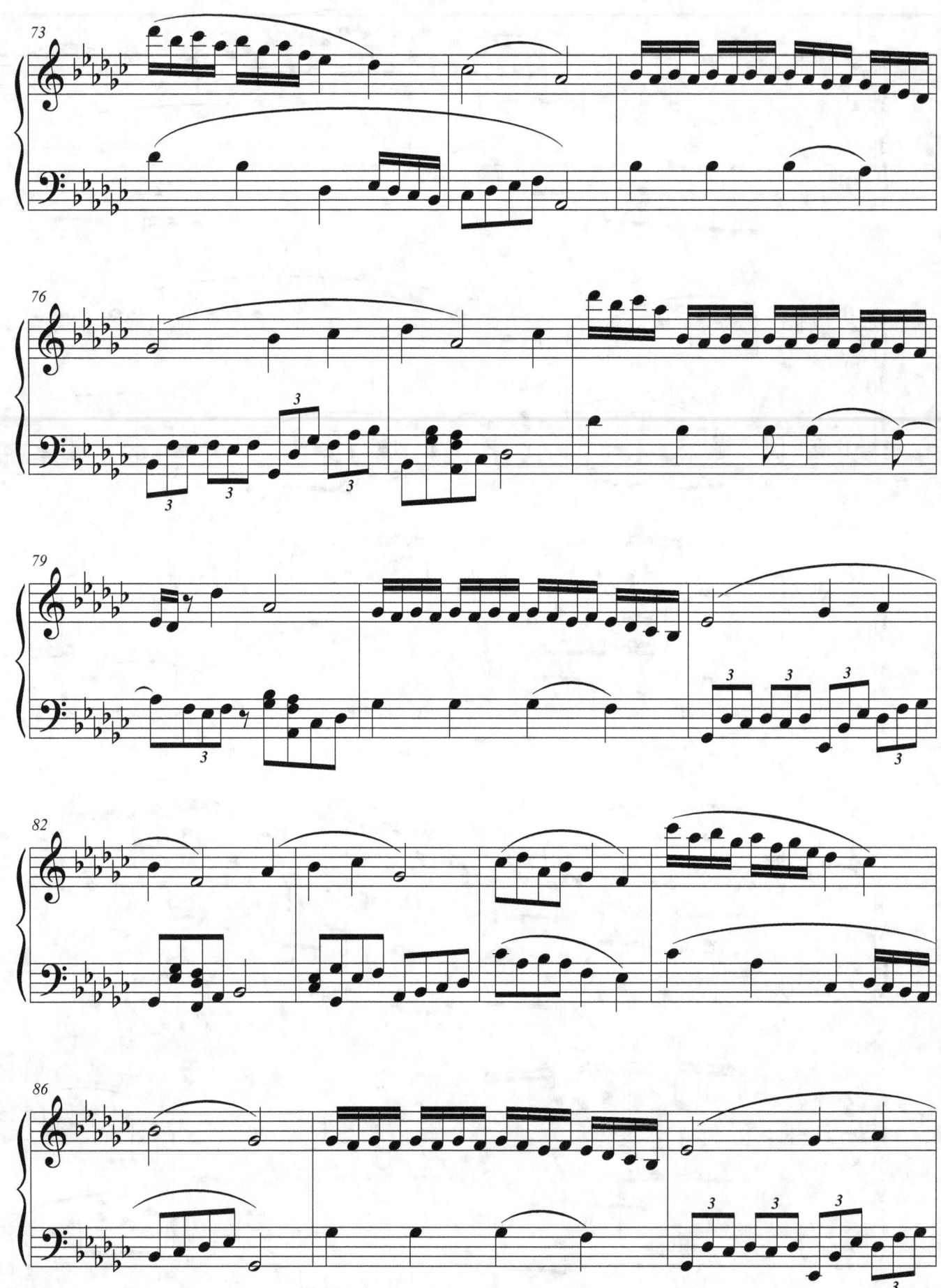

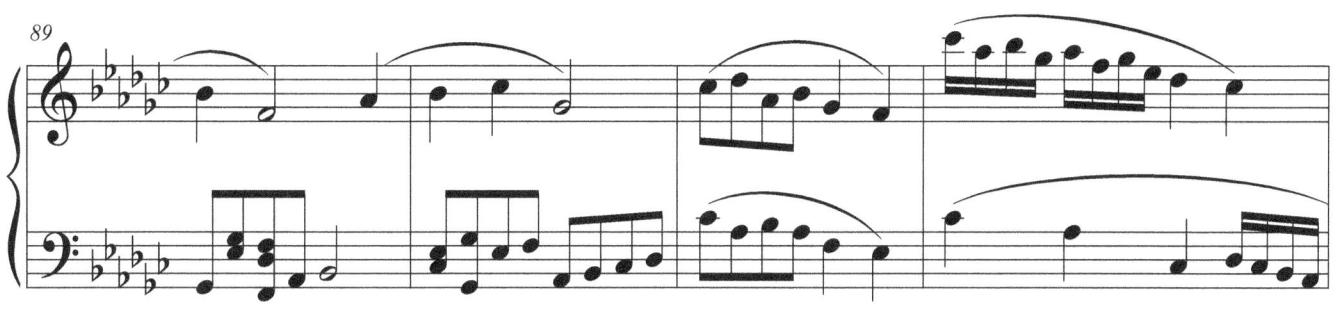

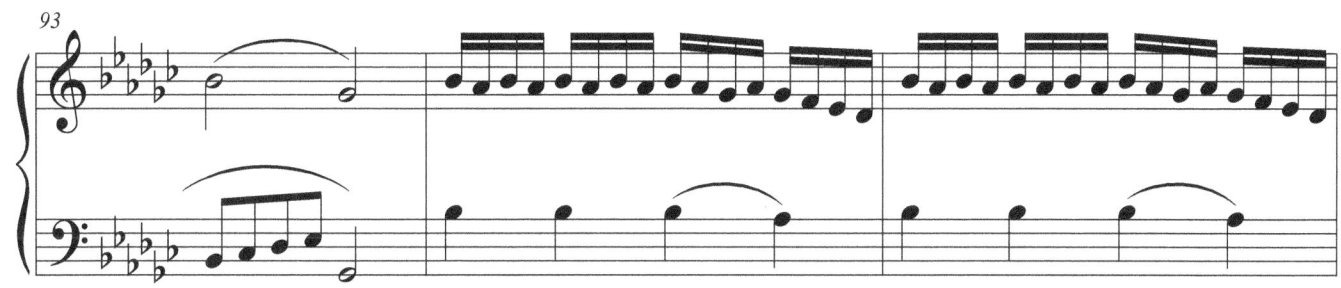

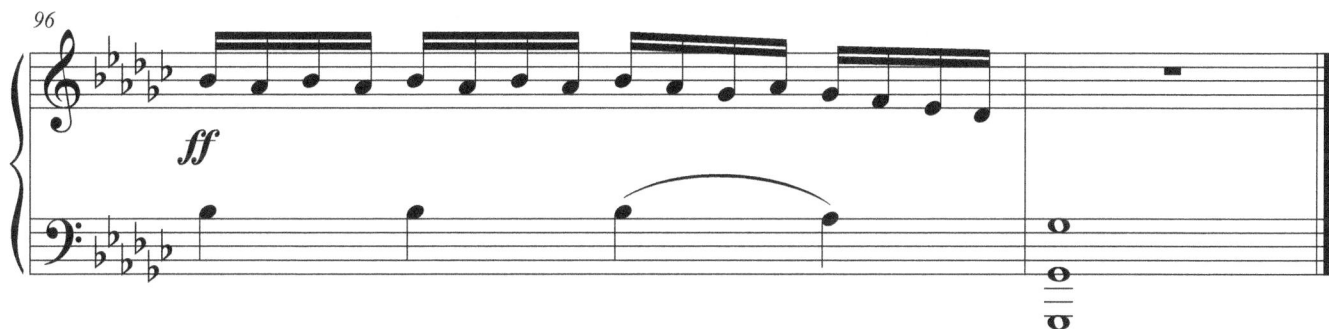

Prelude No.7

De Zarraga Lago, Dubiell, A.

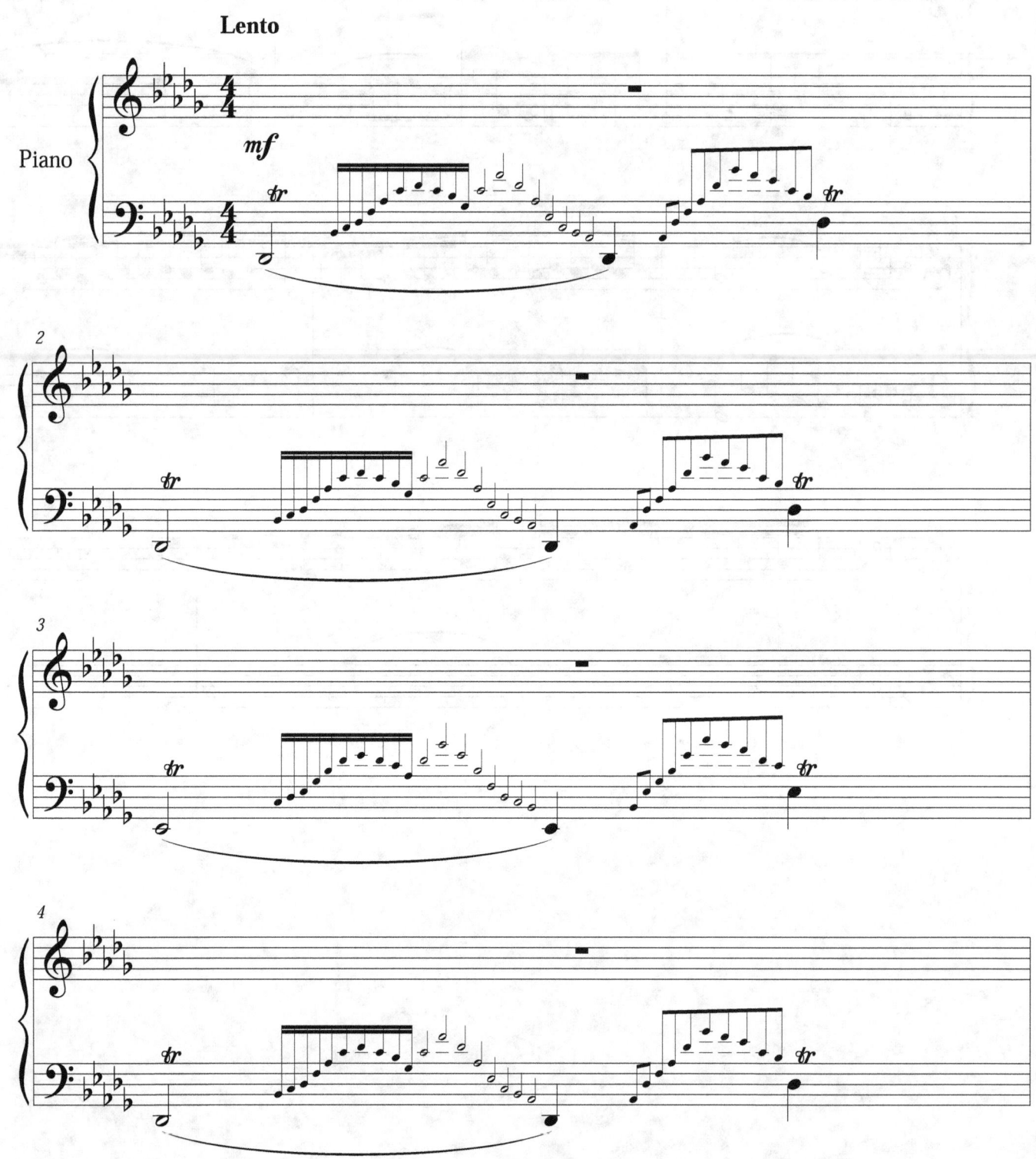

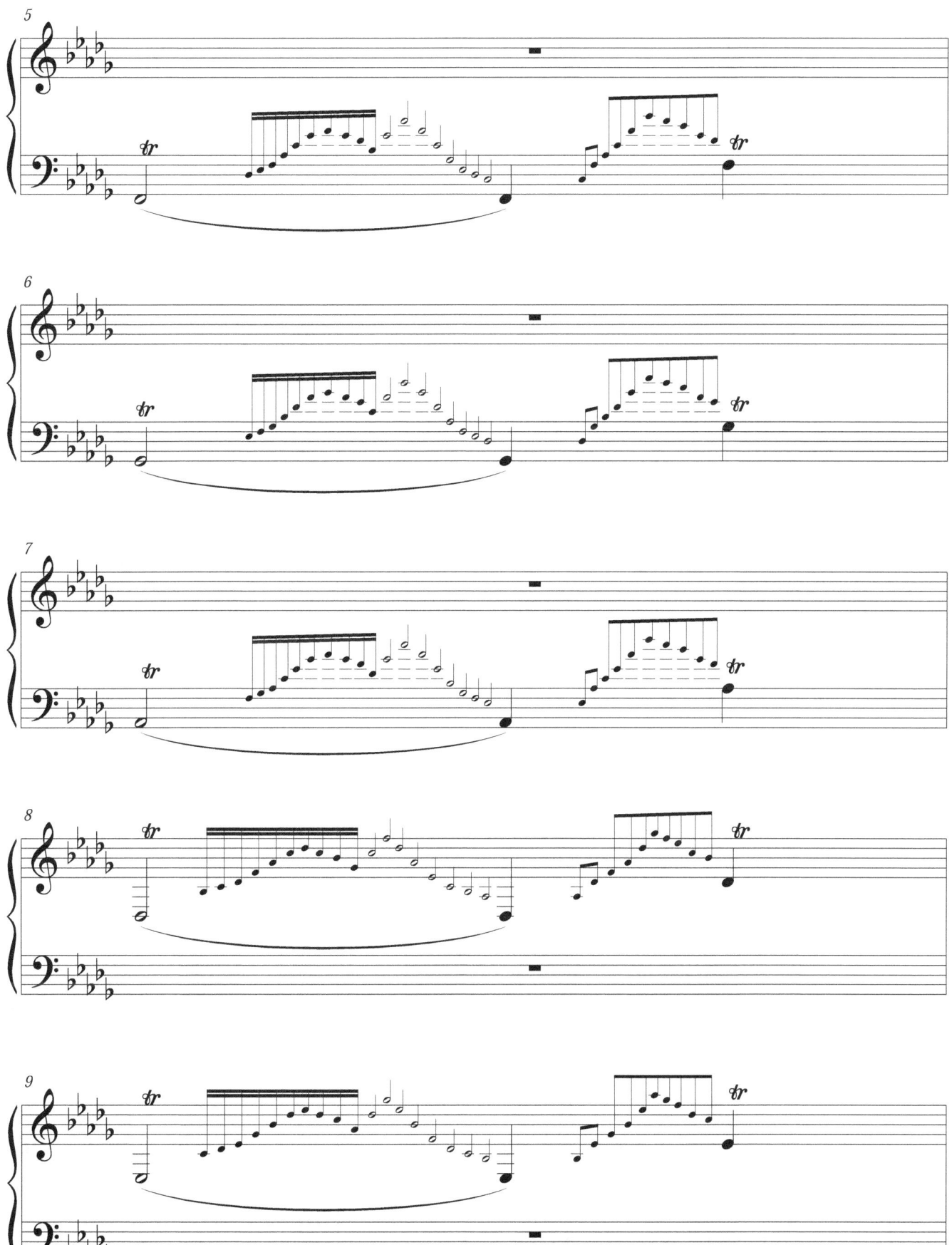

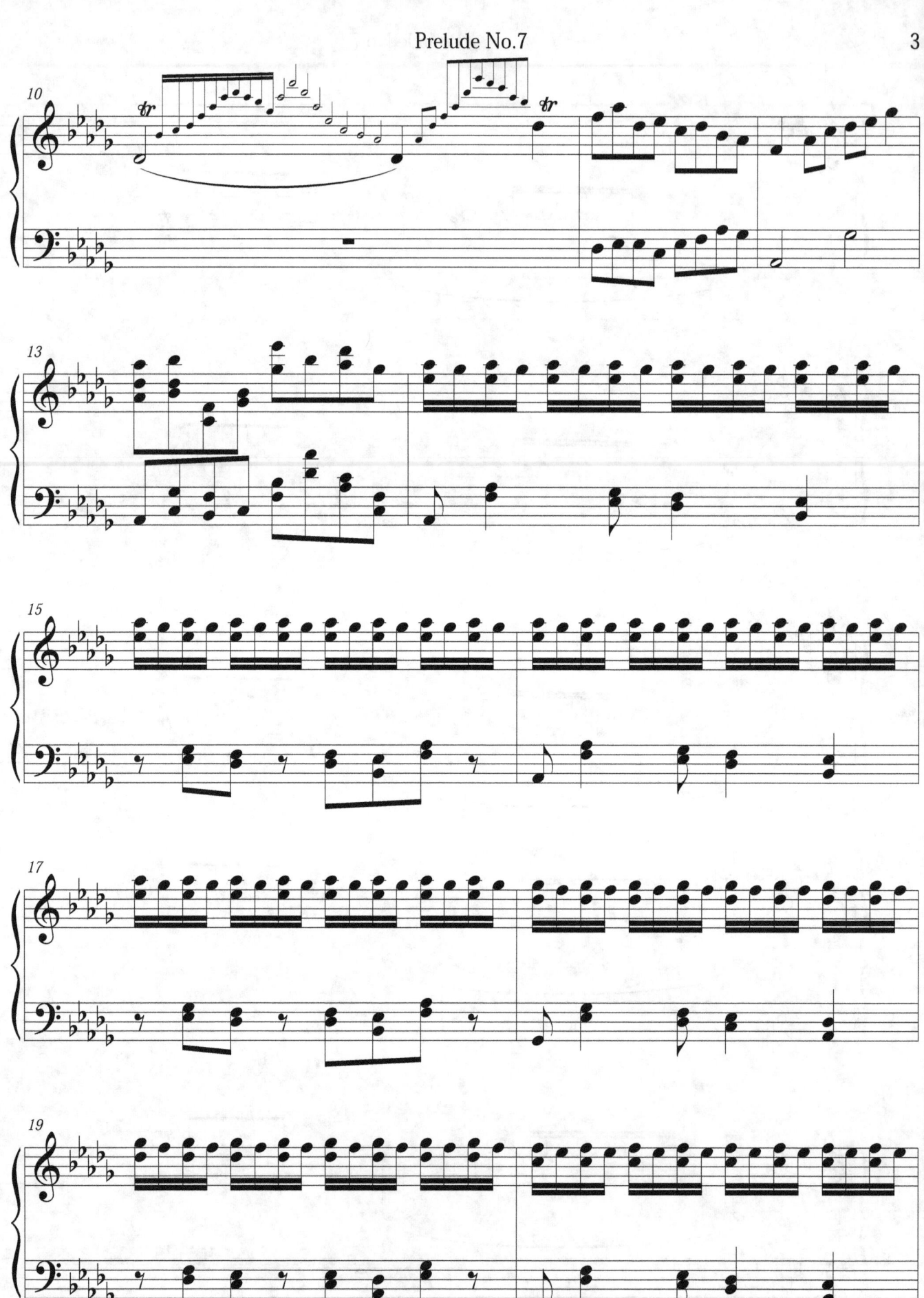

Prelude No.7

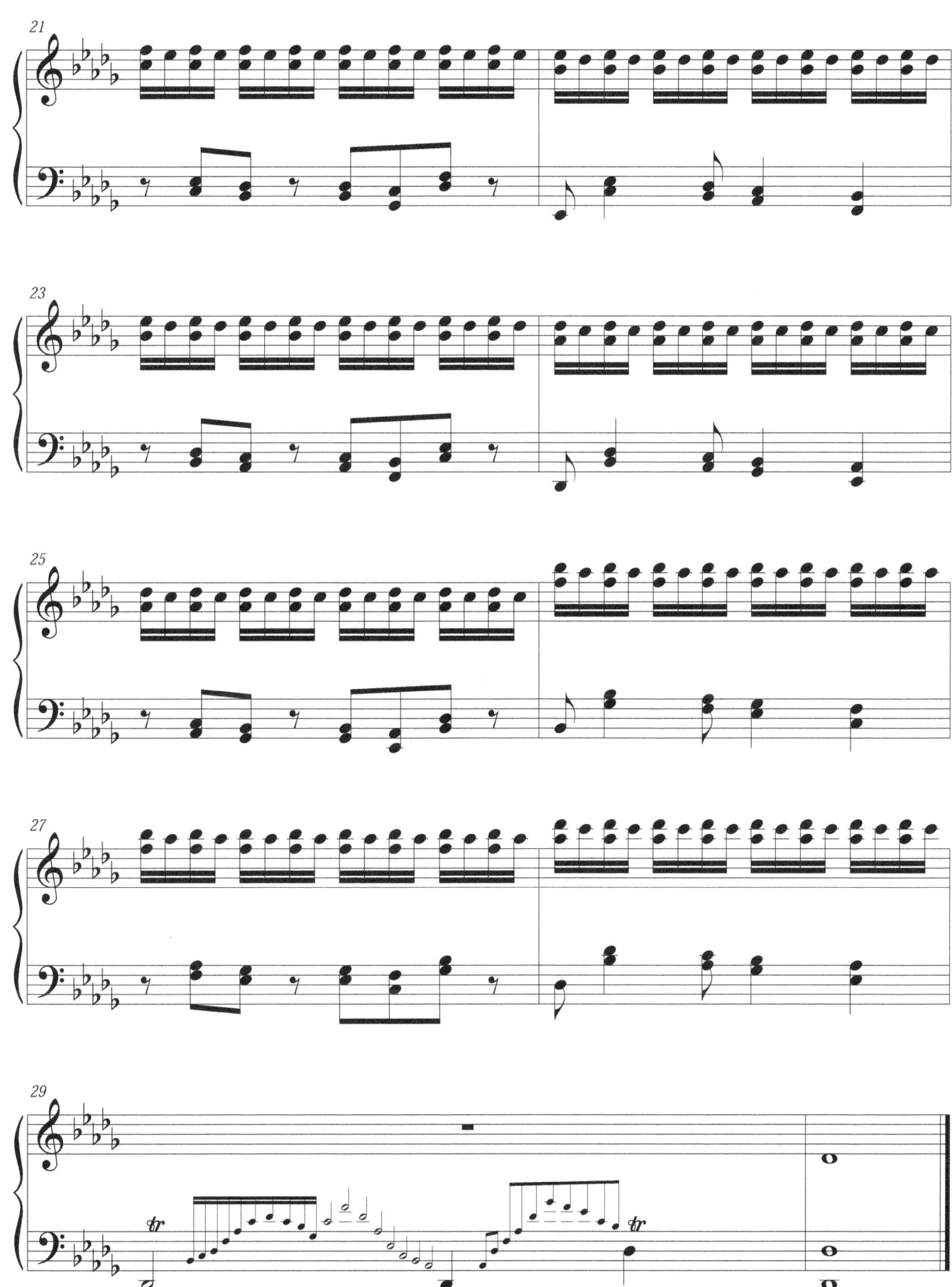

Prelude No.8

Dubiell De Zarraga Lago

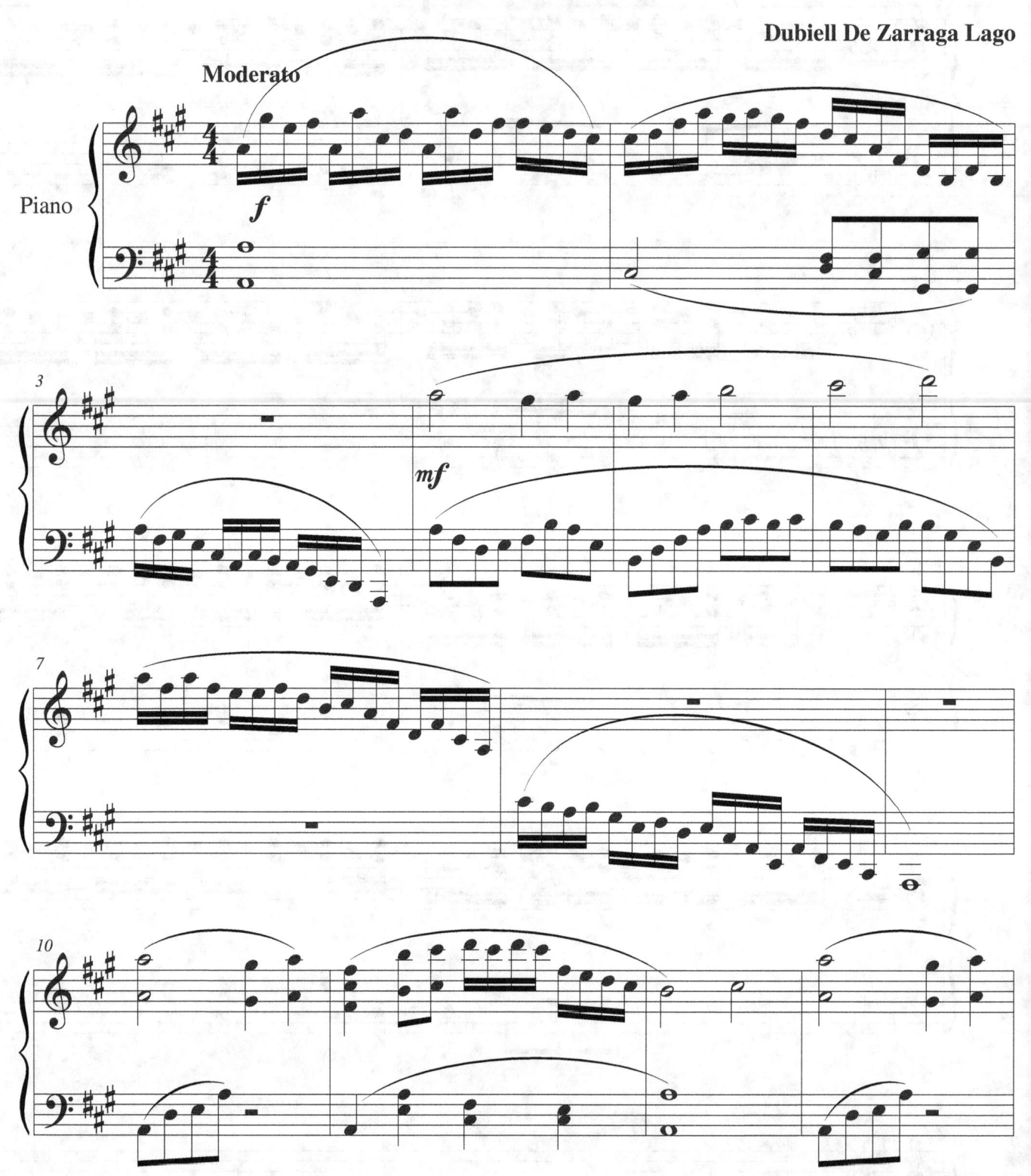

Prelude No.8

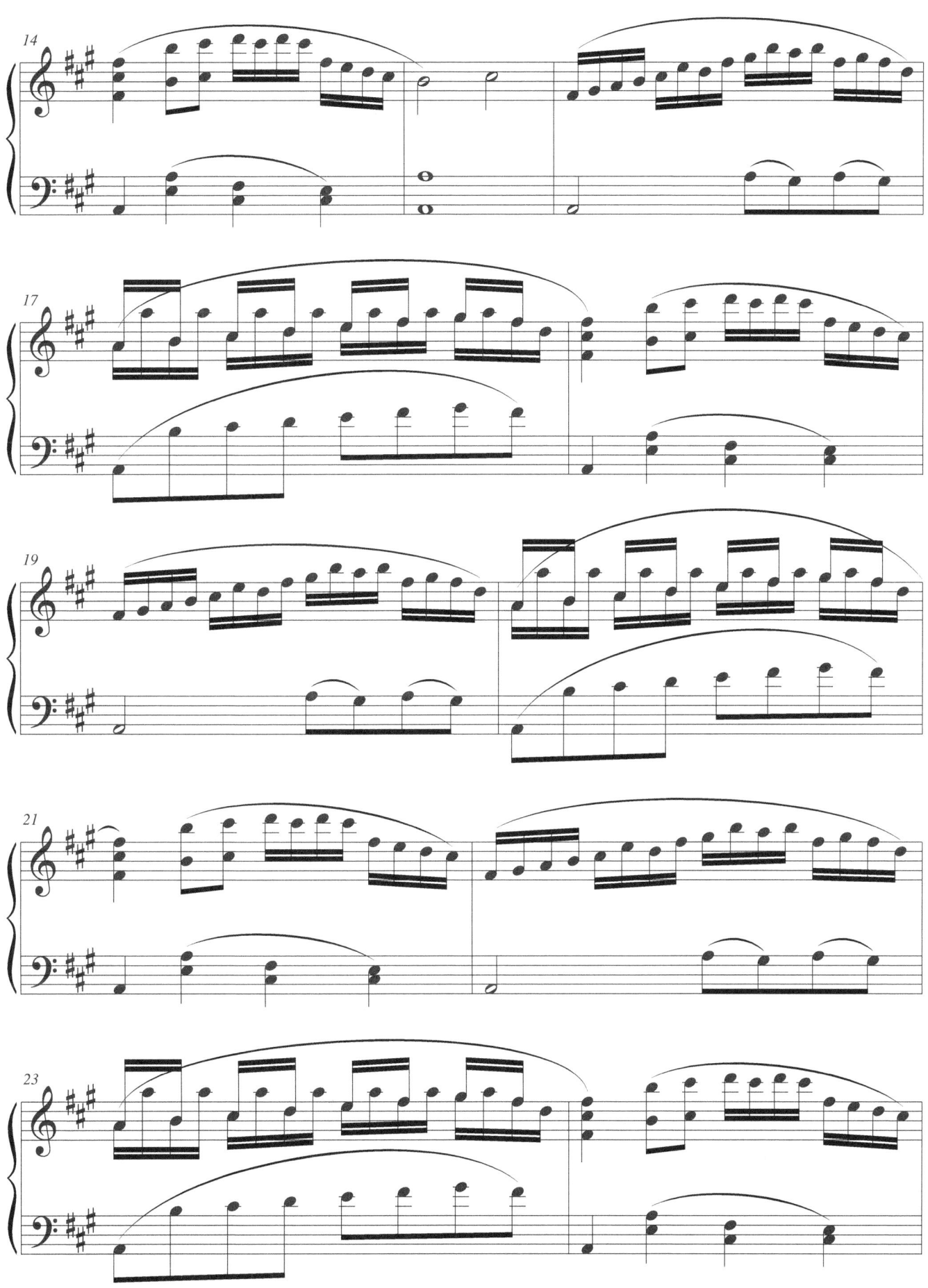

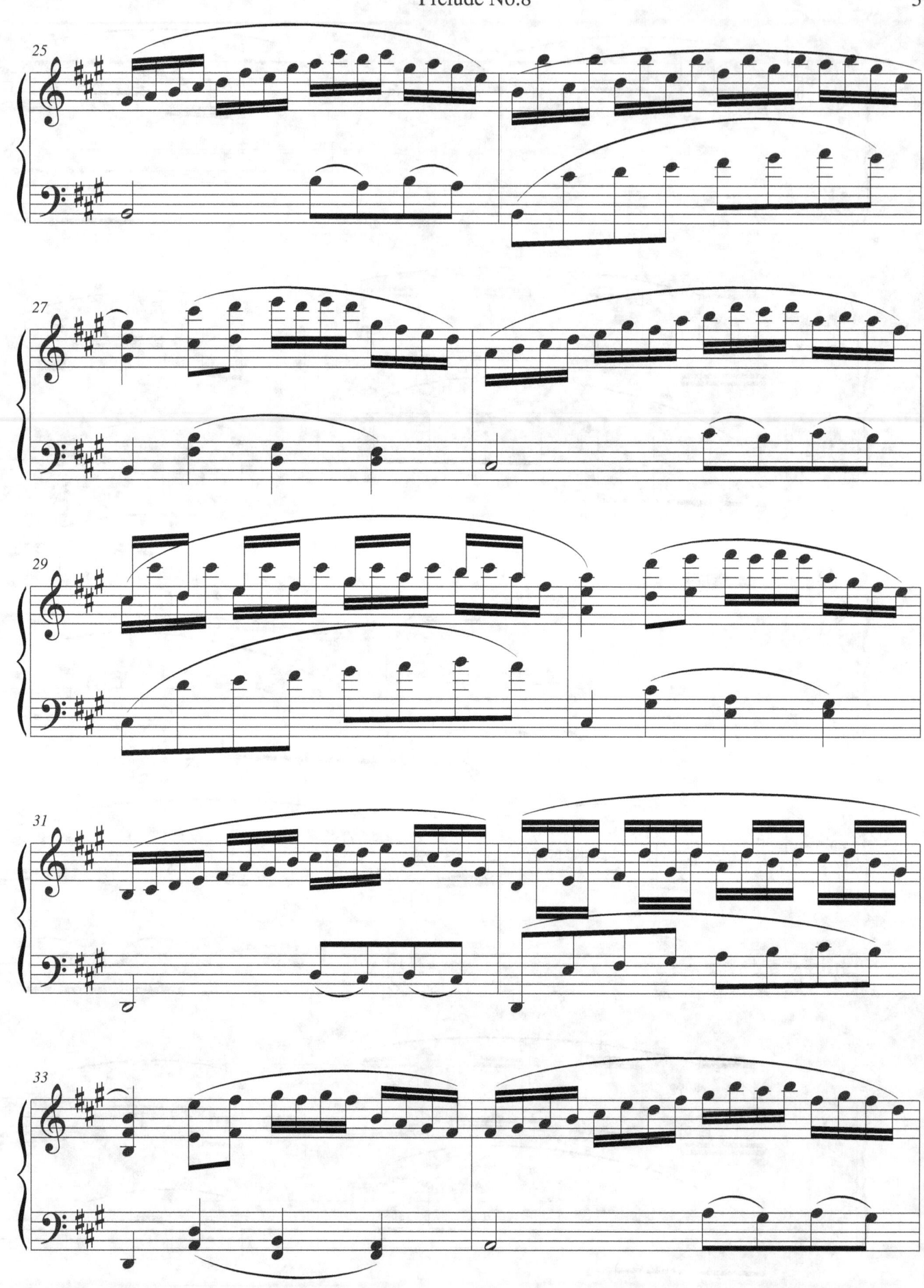

Prelude No.8

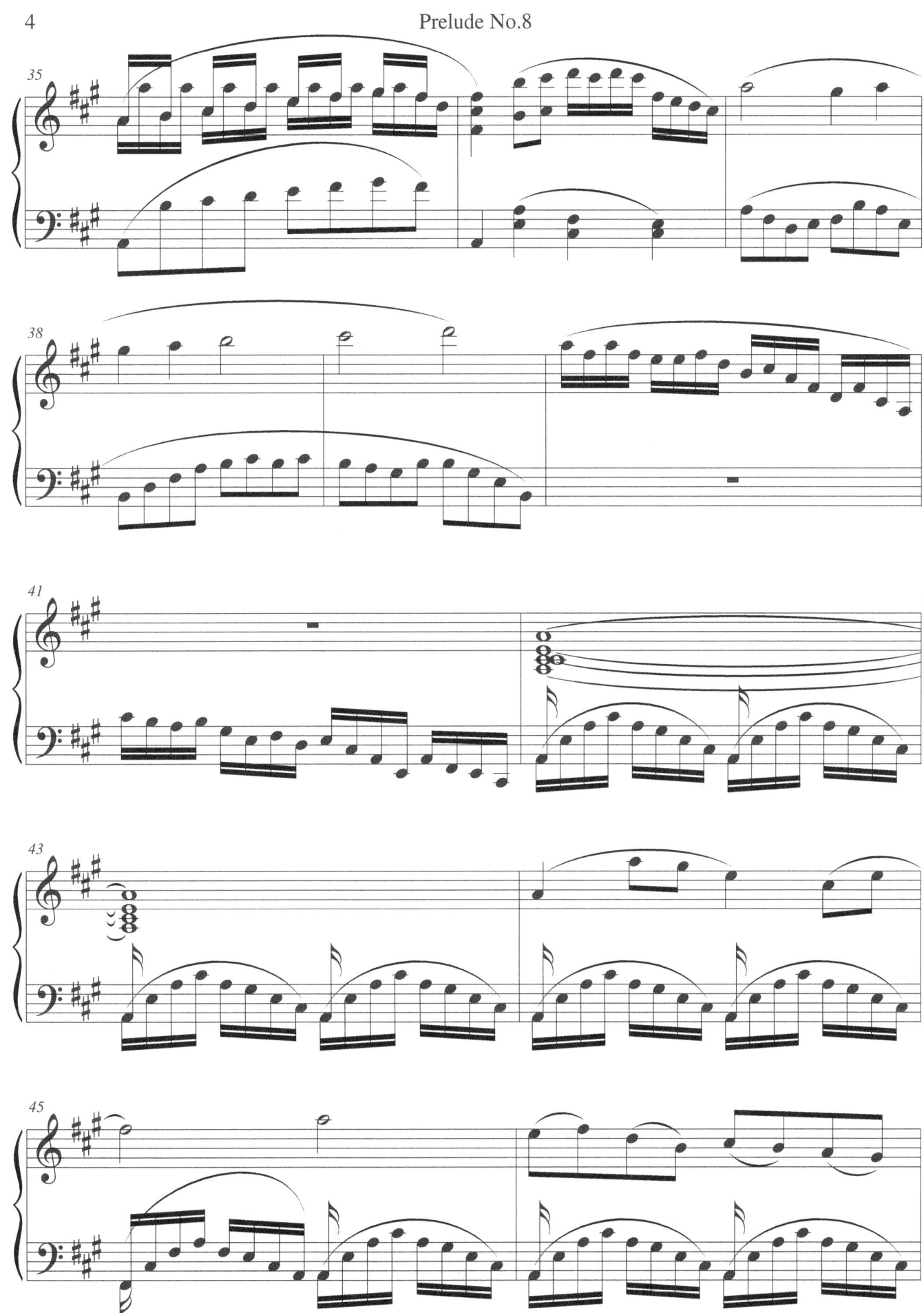

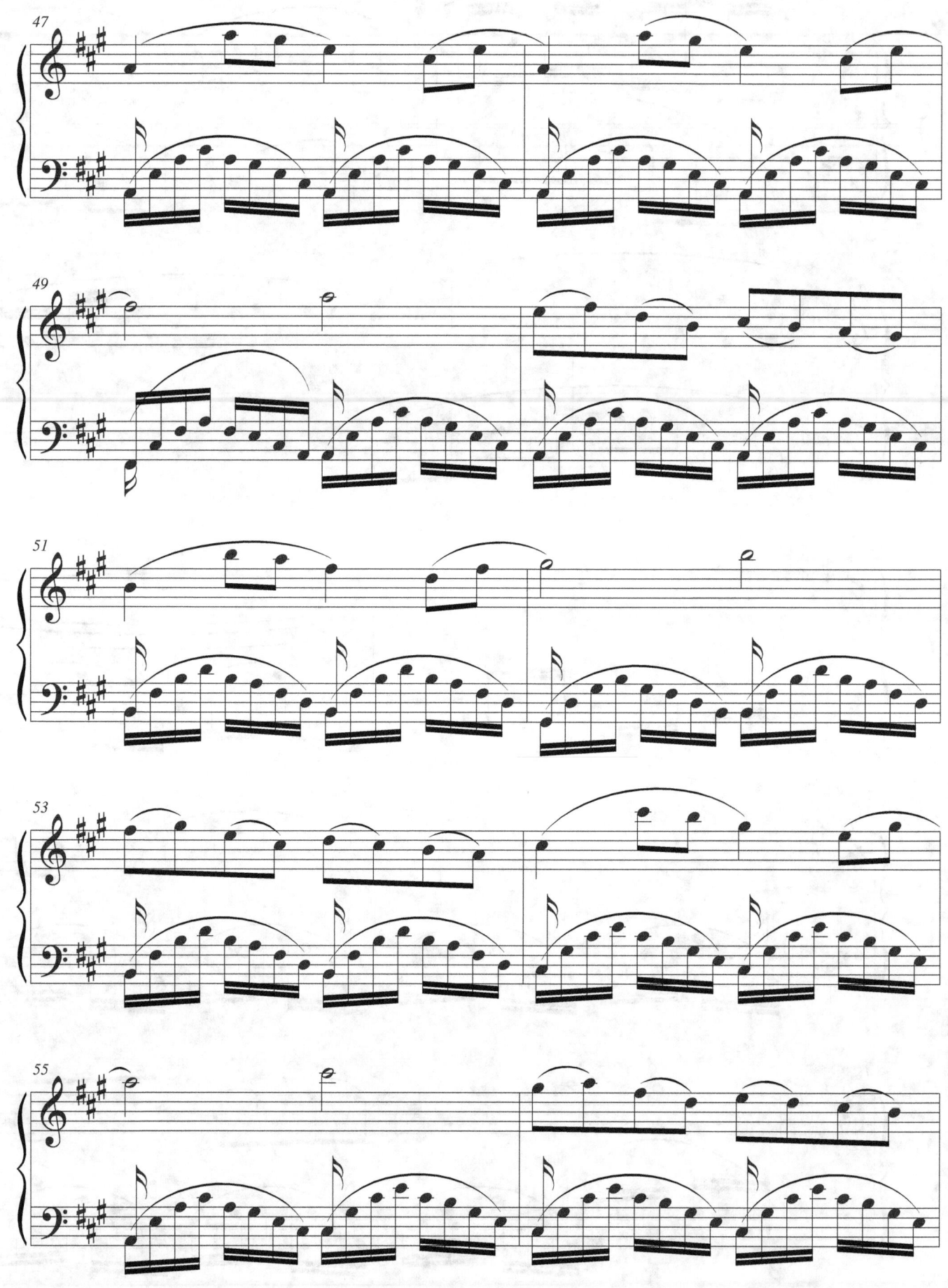

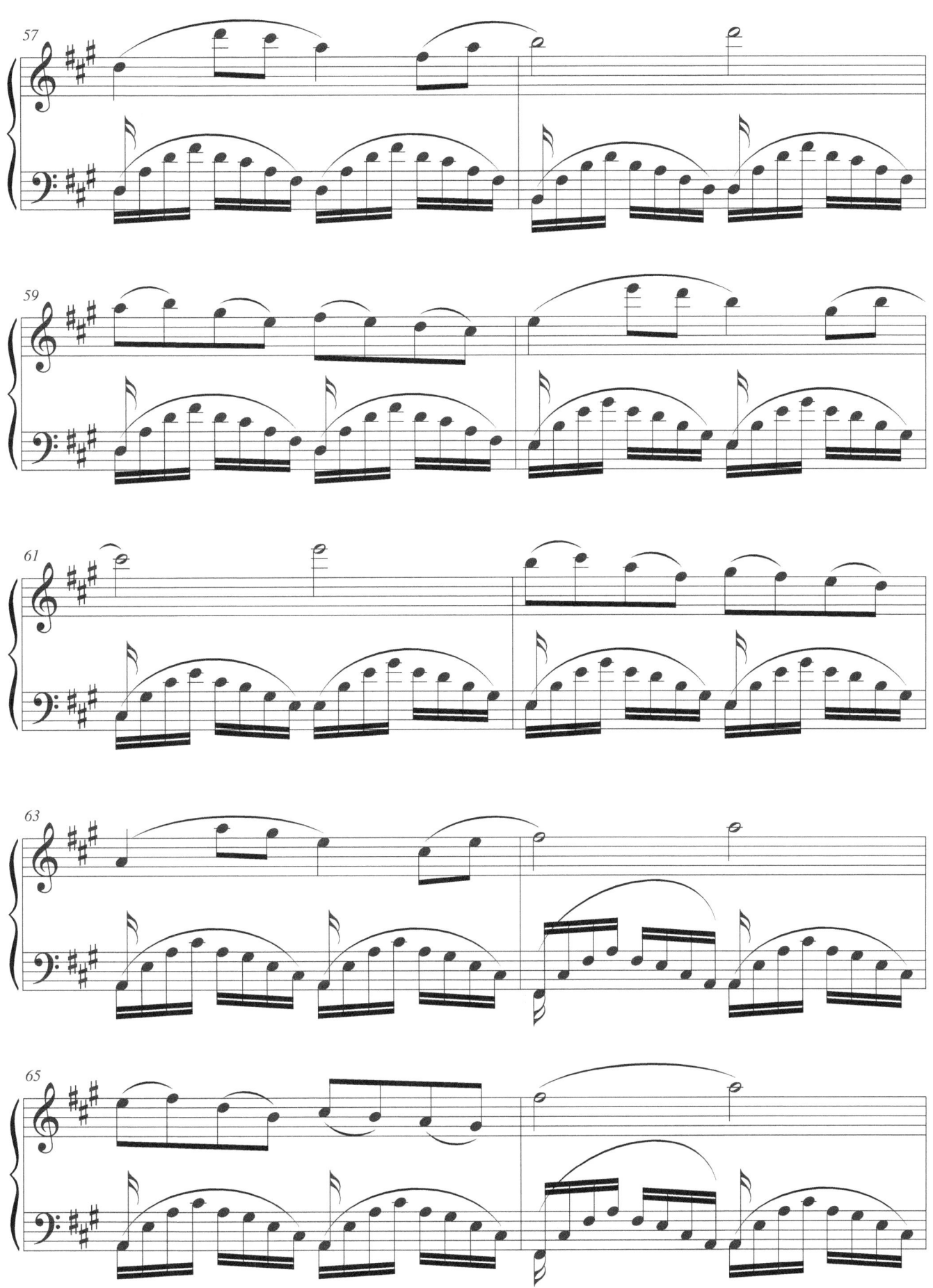

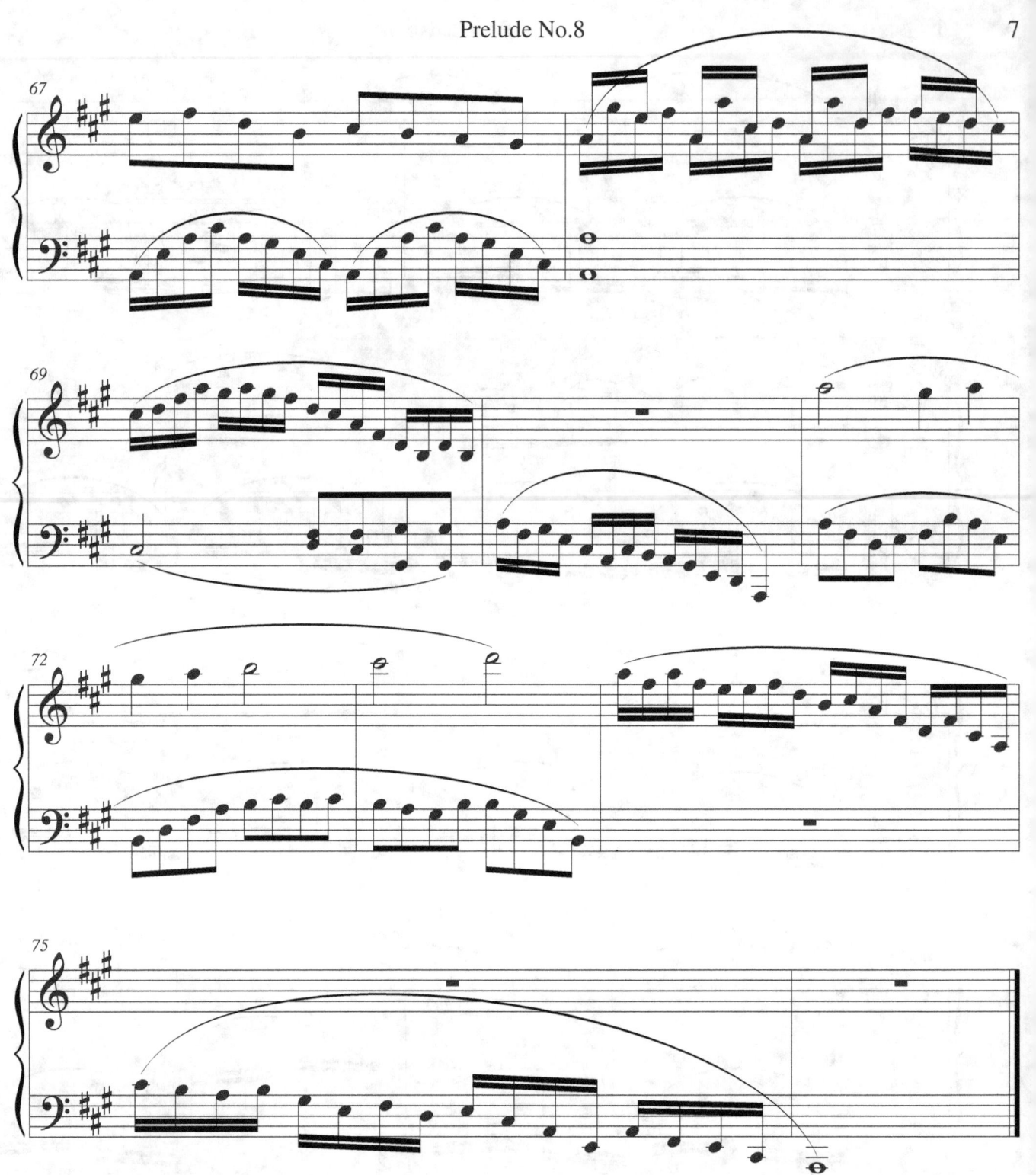

Prelude No.9

Dubiell De Zarraga Lago

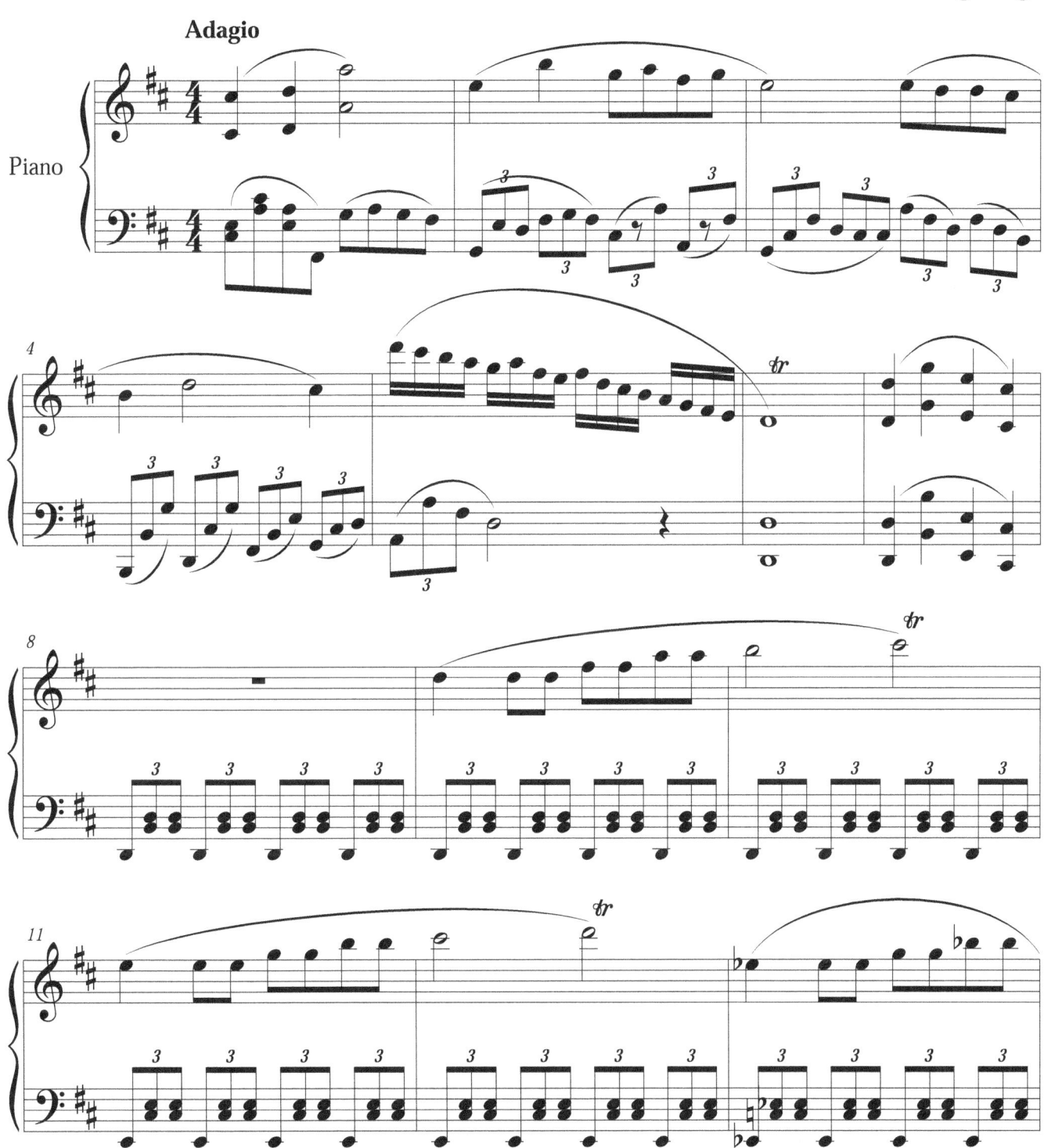

Prelude No.9

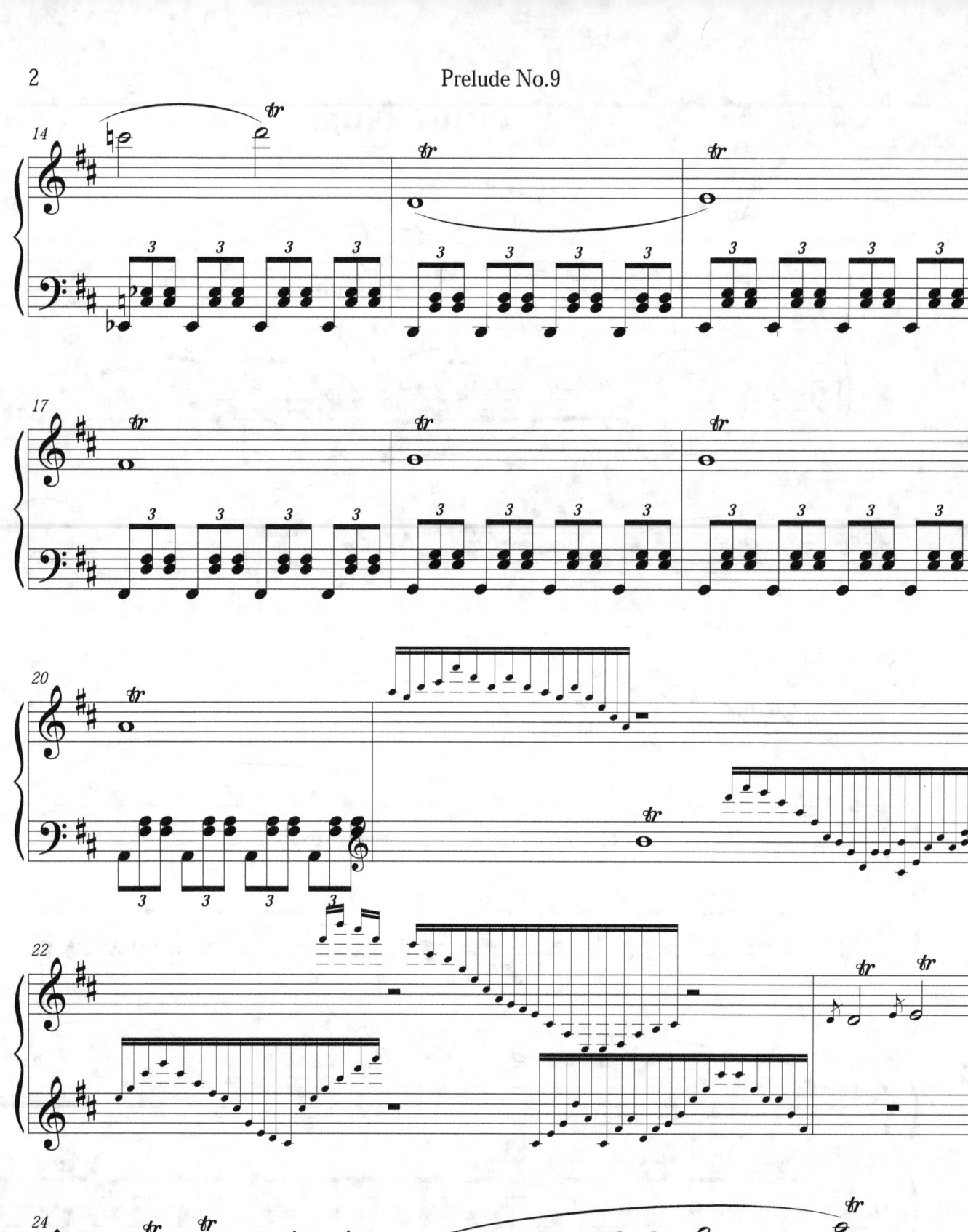

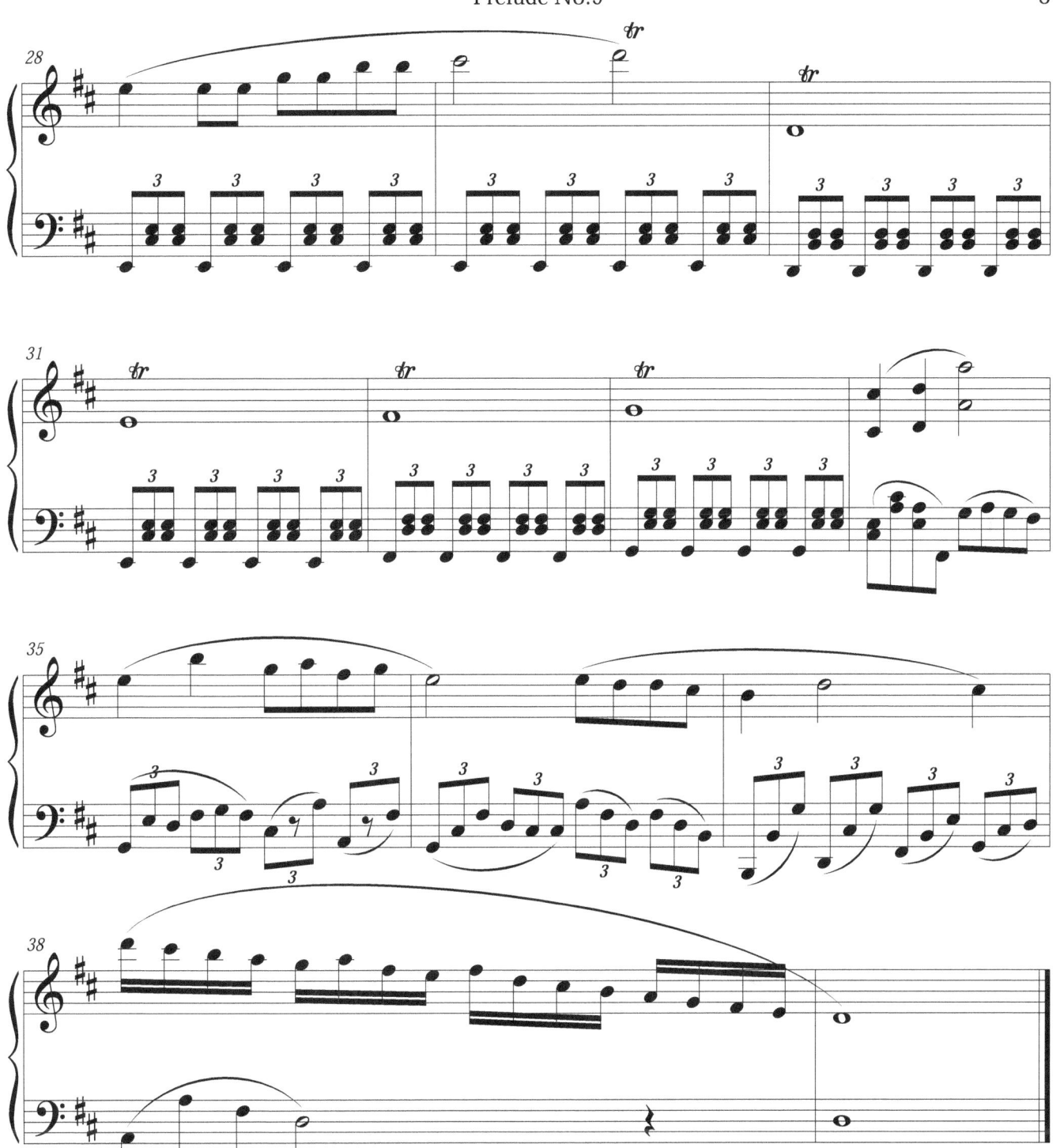

Prelude No.10

Dubiell De Zarraga Lago

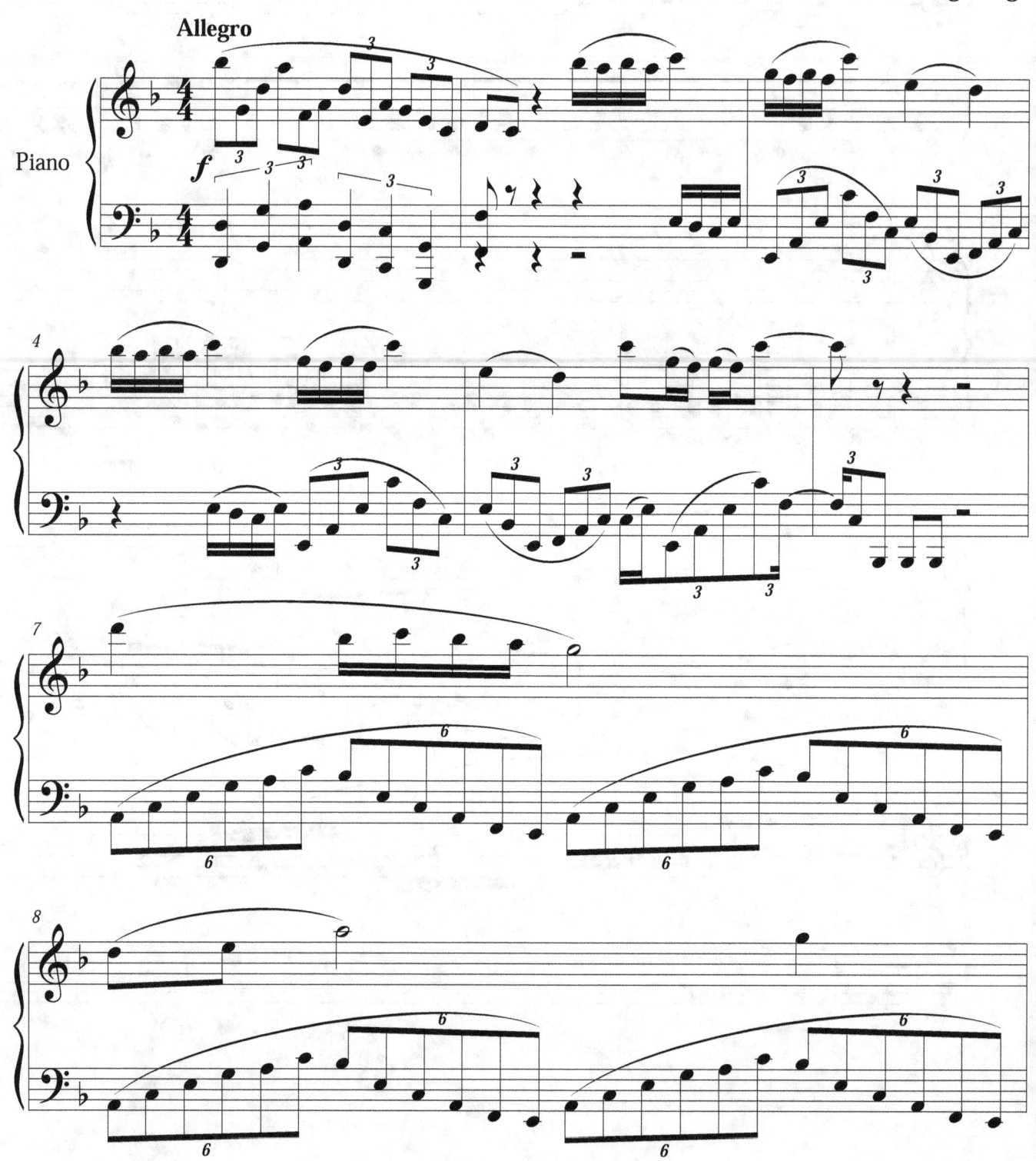

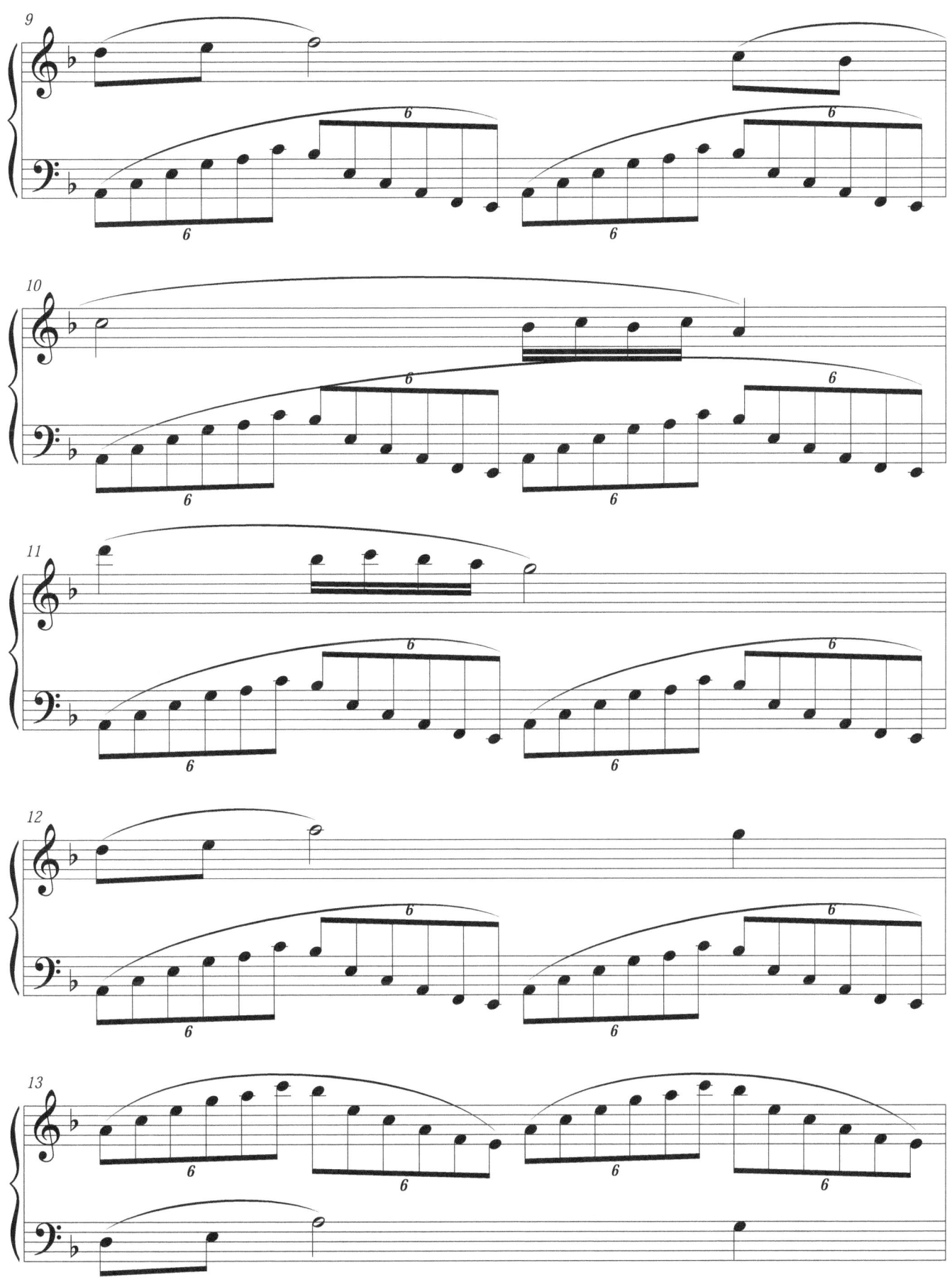

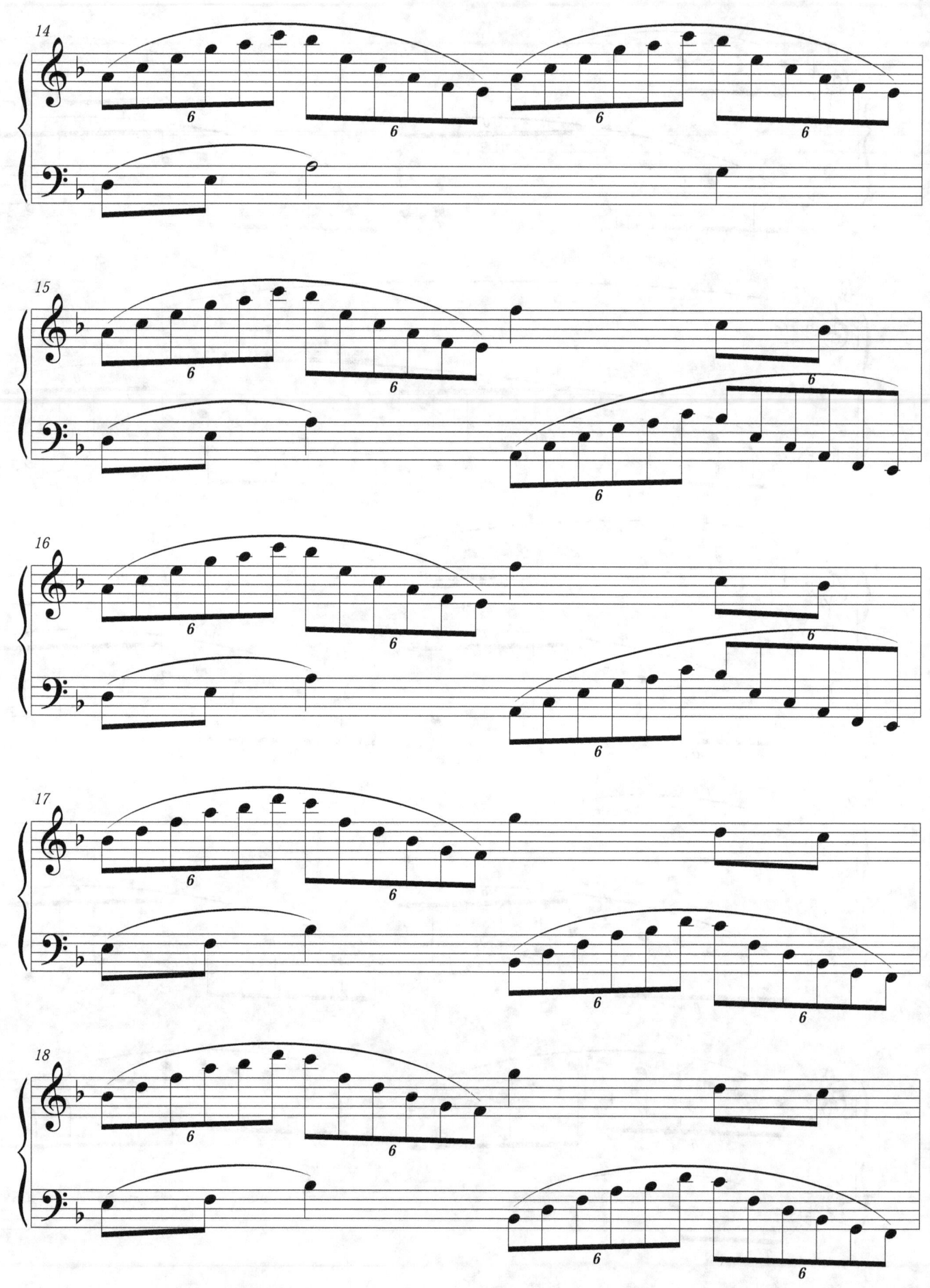

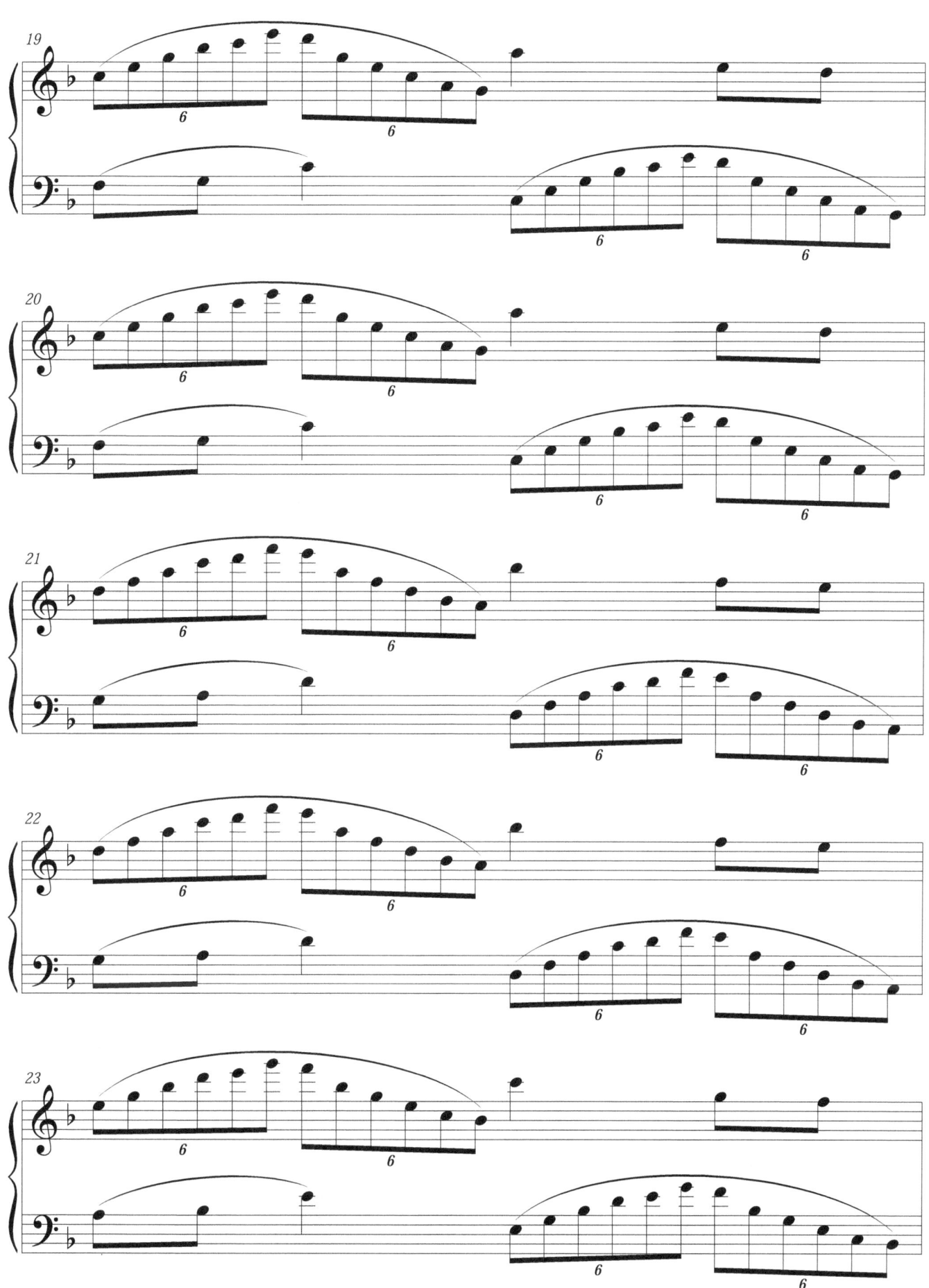

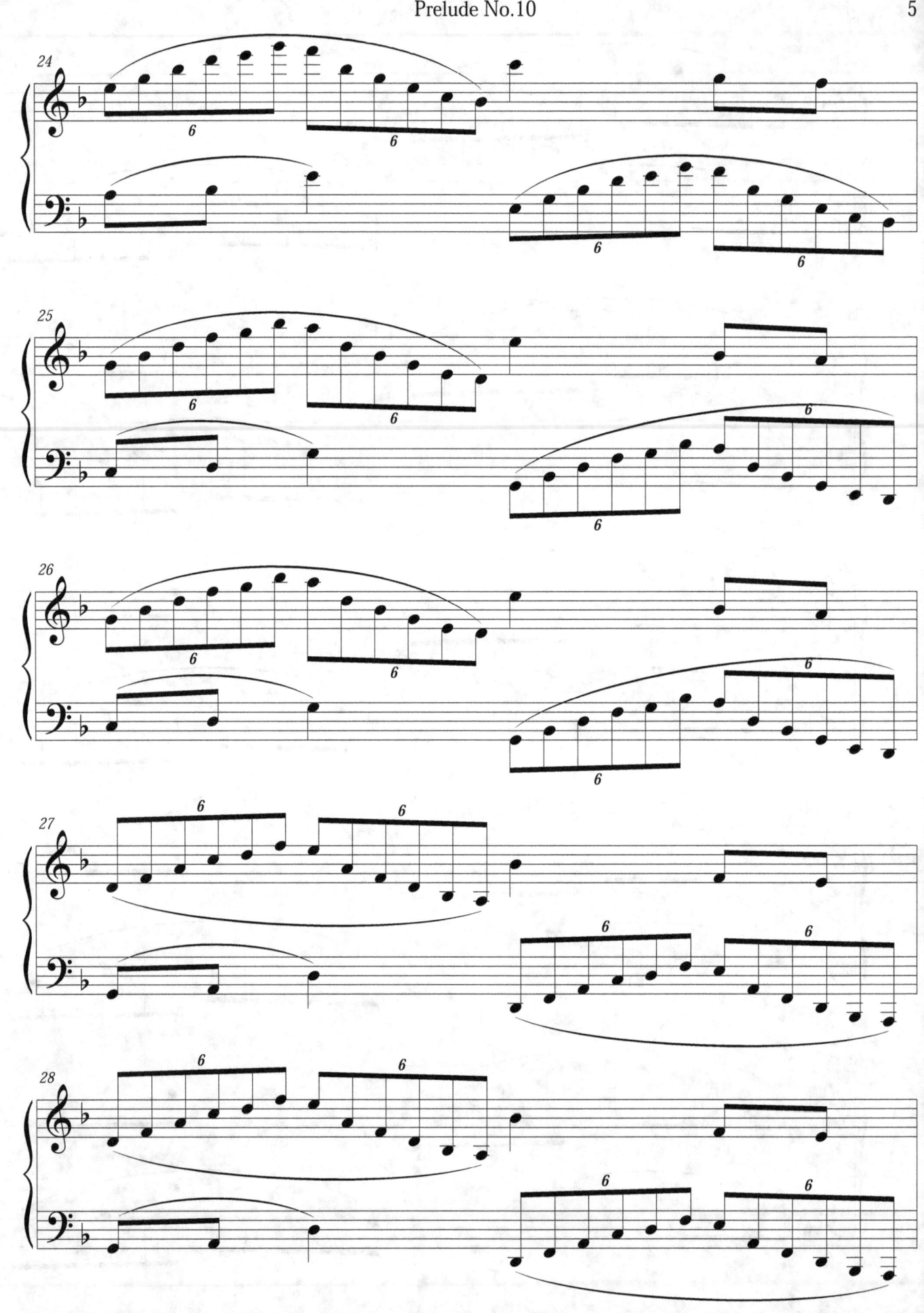

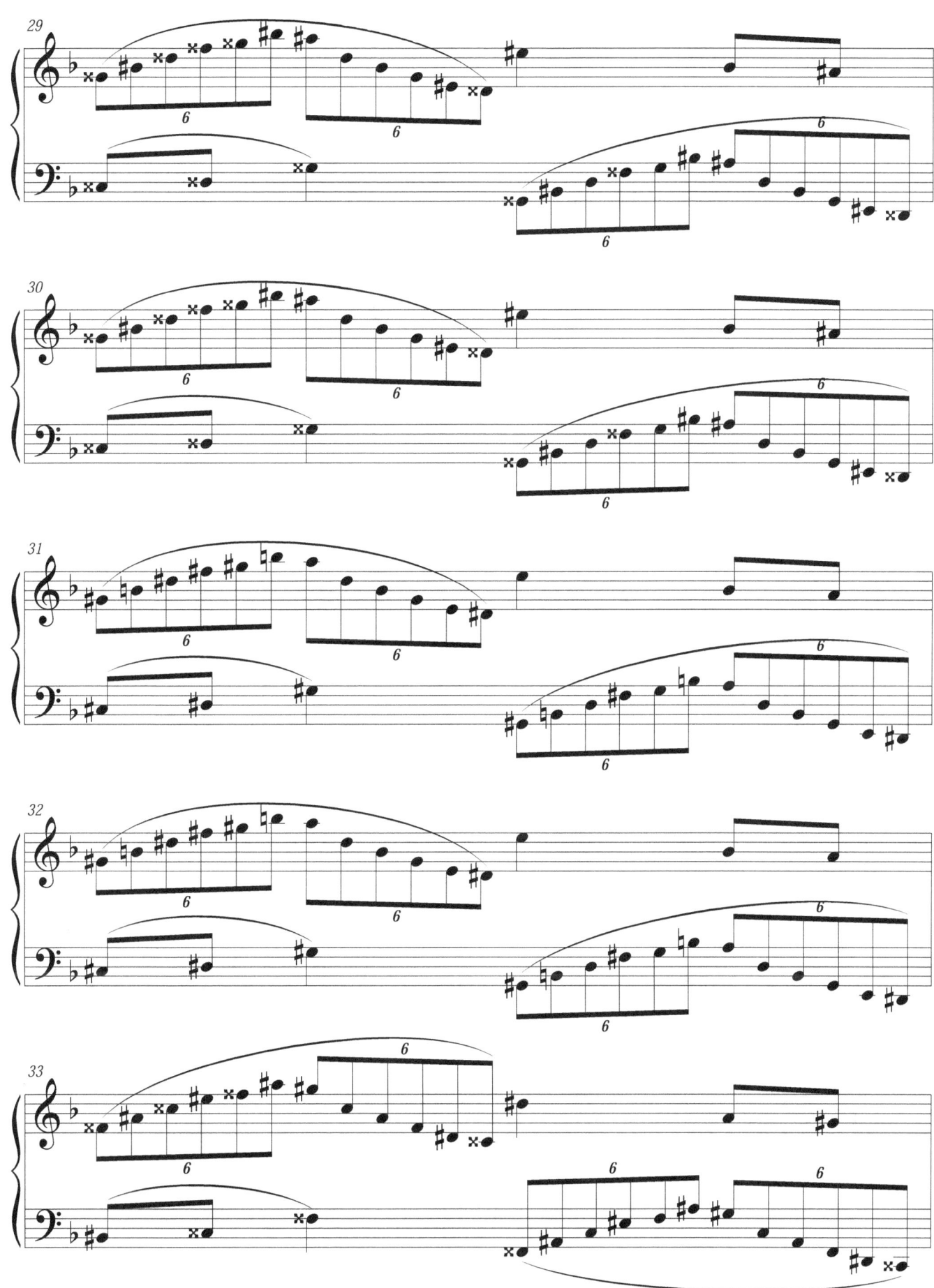

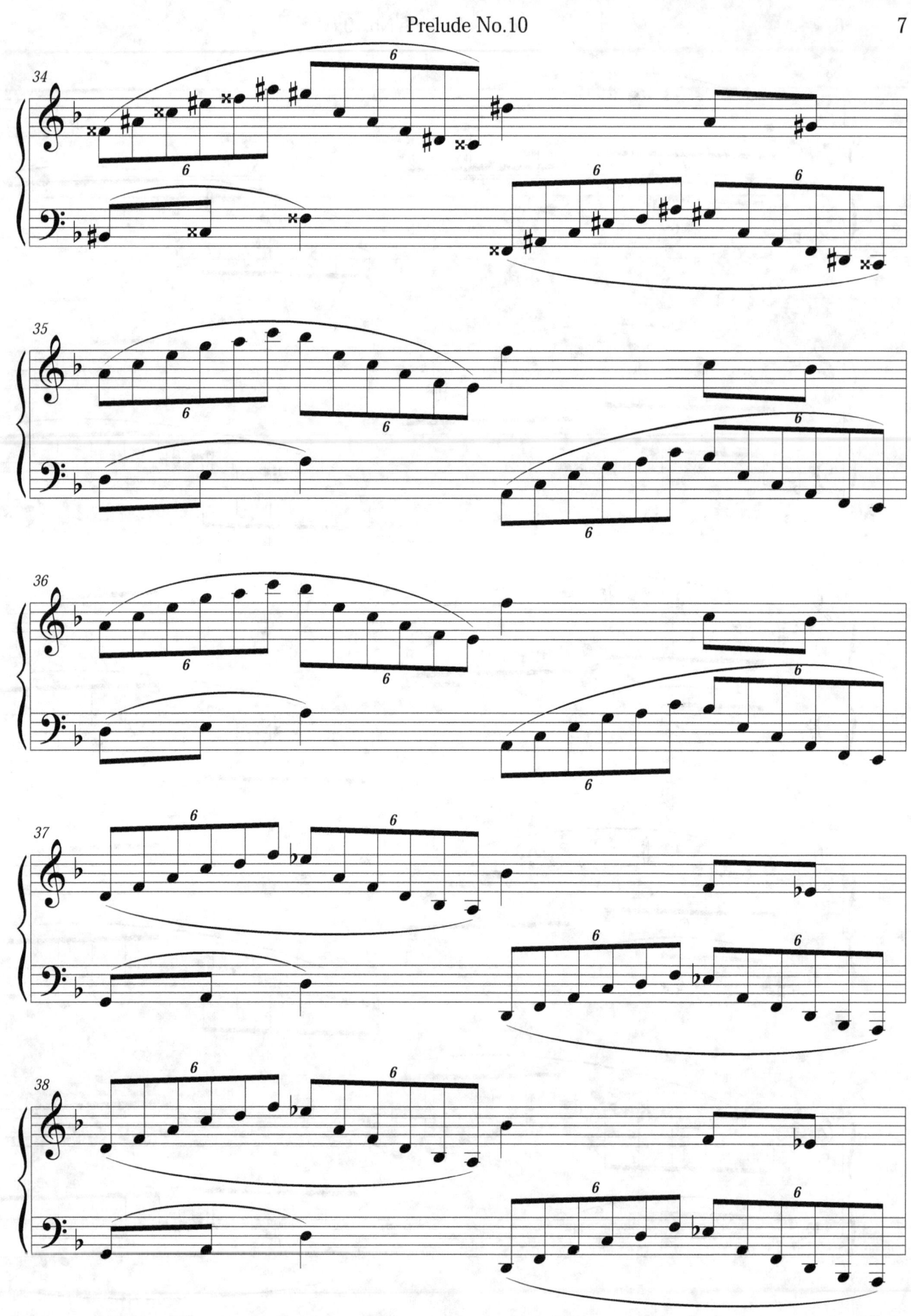

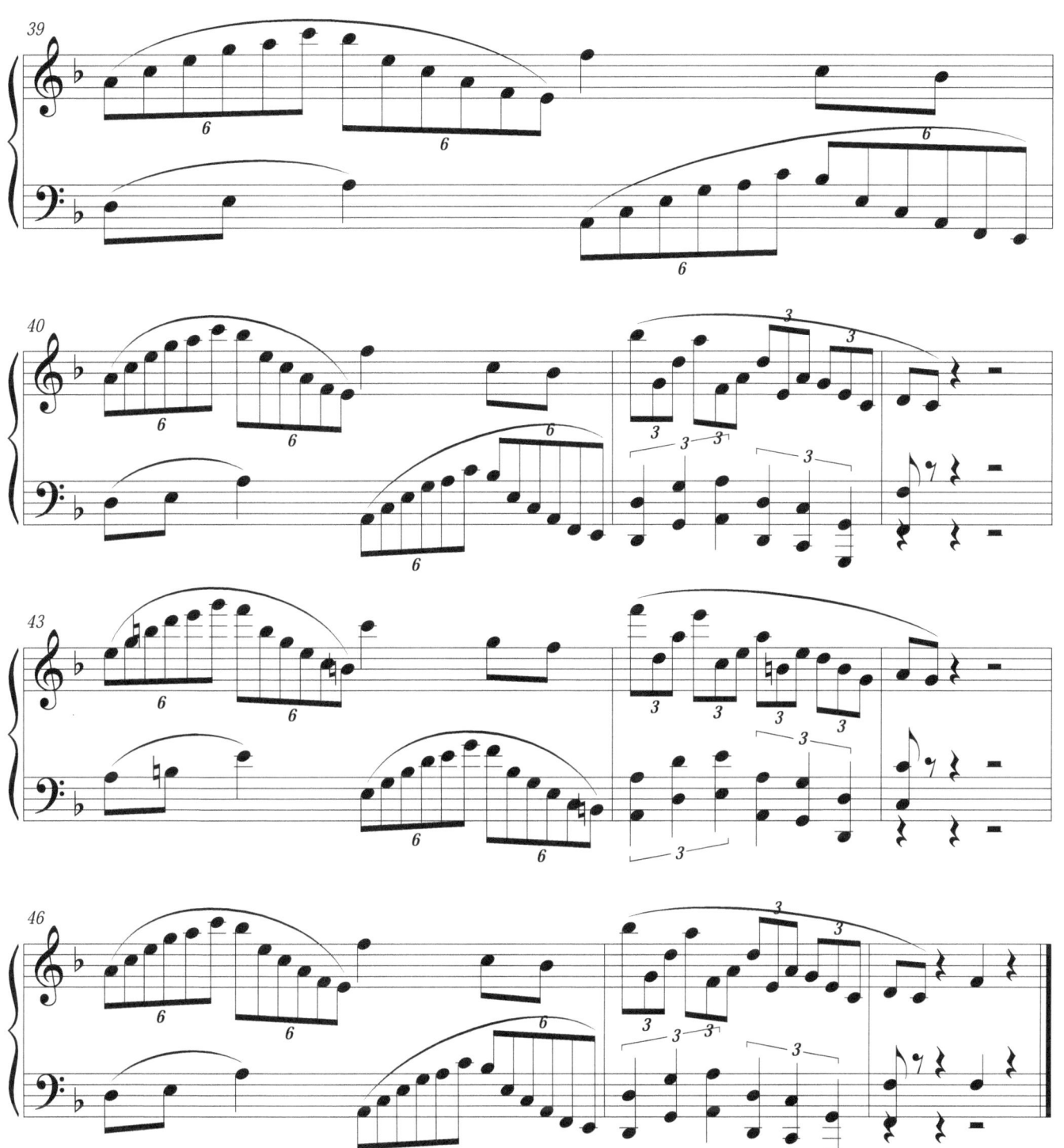

Other Works

Etudes

Etude No. 1
Etude No. 2
Etude No. 3
Etude No. 4
Etude No. 5
Etude No. 6
Etude No. 7
Etude No. 8
Etude No. 9
Etude No.10

Etude No.11
Etude No.12
Etude No.13
Etude No.14
Etude No.15
Etude No.16
Etude No.17
Etude No.18
Etude No.19
Etude No.20
Etude No.21

Consolations

Consolation No.1
Consolation No.2
Consolation No.3
Consolation No.4
Consolation No.5
Consolation No.6
Consolation No.7
Consolation No.8
Consolation No.9
Consolation No.10
Consolation No.11
Consolation No.12
Consolation No.13

Rhapsodies

Rhapsody to the Moon
Rhapsody Alabaresque
Rhapsody in C Major

Concertos

Flute Concerto No.1
String Concerto No.1
String Concerto No.2
String Concerto No.3
Piano Concerto No.1

Preludes

www.lulu.com/dubiell

www.dezarragadubiell@yahoo.com

Notes